DATA-DRIVEN MARKETING CONTENT: A PRACTICAL GUIDE

Praise for *Data-driven Marketing Content: A Practical Guide*

Lee has been my go-to guy for search marketing advice for almost five years now, and I don't see that changing any time soon. He has an encyclopaedic knowledge of search engine optimisation (SEO), is obsessed with detail and knows exactly how to explain his innovative techniques – and the benefits of them – clearly and concisely.

*(**Graeme Parton** – Freelance Copywriter and Journalist)*

I had the absolute pleasure of working with Lee in his capacity as Head of SEO at a leading search agency. His passion for delivering content driven search and digital strategies is second to none, as is his passion for creating content that works, sells and delivers value. If you're struggling to make content work for your business or clients, read this book. Better still, talk to Lee.

*(**John McMurray-Williams** – Sales Director – Innovate Creative)*

I have been working with Lee for nearly 10 years in the field of SEO at a leading search marketing agency. During that time I've seen Lee, as Head of SEO, build a successful specialist search team and deliver winning SEO strategies across many clients. The knowledge and experience he has to offer is overwhelming, and there is much, seasoned digital marketers or new, can learn from him.

*(**Dave Colgate** – Senior SEO Specialist – Vertical Leap)*

DATA-DRIVEN MARKETING CONTENT: A PRACTICAL GUIDE

LEE WILSON

United Kingdom – North America – Japan – India – Malaysia – China

Emerald Publishing Limited
Howard House, Wagon Lane, Bingley BD16 1WA, UK

First edition 2019

Reprints and permissions service
Contact: permissions@emeraldinsight.com

British Library Cataloguing in Publication Data
A catalogue record for this book is available from the British Library

ISBN: 978-1-78973-818-6 (Print)
ISBN: 978-1-78973-817-9 (Online)
ISBN: 978-1-78973-819-3 (Epub)

Printed and bound by CPI Group (UK) Ltd, Croydon, CR0 4YY

ISOQAR certified
Management System,
awarded to Emerald
for adherence to
Environmental
standard
ISO 14001:2004.

Certificate Number 1985
ISO 14001

INVESTOR IN PEOPLE

This book is dedicated to the four people who never fail to motivate, inspire and drive me towards all achievements in life: my wife Ayako, daughter Sophia, and parents Cynthia and Douglas.
This is also written for and dedicated to the memory of family members lost over the past few years.

Table of Contents

List of Figures

Author Biography

Lee Wilson (BA Hons) has worked in digital marketing, delivering thousands of integrated content and marketing campaigns since 2003, after he successfully graduated from Winchester University, England, UK, with honours in Business Management and Communications.

Lee is a Certified Web Applications Developer through the Open University (Cert WAD), individually Google Analytics (GA) qualified and has Search Engine Marketing Professional qualifications (SEMPO) relevant to the authoring of this book.

For the past number of years, Lee Wilson has been employed as Head of Enterprise SEO for a top 10 UK Search and Digital marketing agency (Vertical Leap). During that time, he has worked on and led huge numbers of data-driven campaigns within search marketing, digital and content niches, spanning leading global brands, start-ups, SMEs, plus new entrepreneurial ventures.

Prior to working in the agency side of marketing, Lee Wilson was employed in-house for over seven years as the marketing head and leader of direct and digital marketing departments. Lee took the step towards setting up and running his own digital content and marketing business in 2008.

Personally, Lee is a passionate author (his first solely authored book was published in 2016 – *Tactical SEO: The Theory and Practice of Search Marketing*), has vast experience and insights covering many marketing specialist areas and has been mentally ideating and developing this body of work into this business guide since working on his first few websites back at the start of the 2000s when his interest in this realm was sparked.

As an industry expert, Lee Wilson can be seen providing expert opinion and content contribution to many influential websites and businesses including being regularly cited on; *Search Engine Journal*, State of Digital, plus a host of other media sites and mainstream publications.

Outside of content, marketing and writing, Lee derives inspiration from his wife, young daughter, mum and dad, plus close friends who inspire him every day, bringing lots of light and love into his life.

Foreword

When I first started leading digital content and marketing teams in the early 2000s, I quickly acquired a passion for sharing practical advice, expertise and helping others through my experiences.

This has driven me to communicate and distribute my expertise spanning many of the most popular business, search, digital and marketing sites on the Internet.

Over the past 15+ years working in the marketing industry within senior positions, I've had the privilege of driving many hundreds (likely thousands) of integrated marketing projects, cross-channel marketing/content campaigns, ongoing projects and long-term retainer bodies of work.

I have worked with some of the largest international businesses, brand new start-up companies and hundreds of small- to medium-sized businesses (SMBs), all bringing new challenges and opportunities to explore marketing content approaches to deliver increased results.

The most common thread spanning all of this time collaborating with businesses regardless of scale, historical performance or budget, is that business, marketing and wider user content can always deliver more.

In 2016, I created my first solely authored book which has now launched into international audiences (*Tactical SEO: The Theory and Practice of Search Marketing*), and ever since then have been planning to complete this guide, helping businesses and practitioners generate business and marketing content that works.

This book empowers content professionals, marketing teams and practitioners of all industries to take gut feel out of the content creation process and replace it with something much more powerful and effective – data-driven insight.

Throughout this guide, you will be provided with everything you need to take your marketing content to a higher level of contribution towards attaining and exceeding your business goals and objectives.

This guide will improve and grow your data ecosystem to empower more meaningful marketing content creation. You will also be able to identify, understand and strengthen your business marketing content to make every word you produce contribute more towards your aims and company aspirations.

Practical expertise is apportioned spanning the key marketing channels, enabling you to target new and existing users regardless of medium or industry with effective content. Added to this, everything is fuelled by data and expertise.

Common marketing content barriers are explored, plus tips are shared to help you overcome the challenges being faced by most companies, plus you can see how to efficiently evaluate your content progress, set the right benchmarks for your business goals, as well as report on your future content successes.

If you want to solidify your content success, gain ground on the top competing businesses within your market and create unique marketing content differentiation, this book is for you.

Acknowledgements

Throughout my career I have had the opportunity to be mentored directly and through standards setting by truly inspiring business leaders, entrepreneurs and key staff in all levels of organisations.

Upon reflection, a great deal of insight has come from my peers and the people I have had the privilege of managing directly.

At the time of creating this business guide, I took the decision not to name specific people in these acknowledgements, as by doing so I will be omitting direct thanks and appreciation to many others, who without their knowledge, approach and expertise I would not be in the position of creating and sharing this practical content guide today.

Without doubt, most of the knowledge I've gleaned over the years has been as a direct result of discussion (active and passive involvement), and perhaps the most valuable contribution has been made from working in passionate, open and inclusive business cultures.

When a company culture places positive emphasis on knowledge sharing and all staff and service progression, this creates an open and trusted environment stemming creativity, expression and experimentation – all key component parts of effective and continuous improvement.

Thinking back, this business guide began when I worked on my first few websites at the start of the millennium and has been built on with each and every relevant experience since.

By reading this practical data-driven marketing content guide, you will gain a distilled, real-world understanding and fast-tracked insights into the lessons I have learnt, plus the successes achieved over many years in content, digital and marketing senior roles.

Chapter 1

Introducing Data-driven Content

There is more information being collected today than at any other stage during human existence. As you might expect, a substantial amount of this data can be used for enhancing your existing marketing content, plus creating new marketing material that works harder, plus contributing more towards your professional and business goals.

This wealth of new data poses a substantial threat and untapped opportunity for individuals, practitioners and businesses alike, when it comes ideating and producing effective business and marketing content, as well as keeping in touch of the growing online and offline competition.

To put new data growth into context, every minute Google completes 3.6 million searches, 103 billion spam emails are sent and 69 thousand hours of video is streamed on Netflix, and that's just the beginning.

Based on IBM data, 90% of all data available to us today were created in the past two years; this equates to 2.5 quintillion bytes of data created every day, demonstrating the rapid changes in data availability, and the business opportunity to leverage this wealth of ever-increasing data for new insights, actions and a competitive company advantage.

Data-driven Content

Data-driven Marketing Content: A Practical Guide empowers you to identify, understand and act on ever-changing data to make meaning from the deep data dilemma.

Everyone can have access to data-driven insights, which can turn mundane, thinner value content into purposeful, positioned marketing materials created with the user in mind, and is able to deliver results regardless of medium, marketing channel or intended audience.

Businesses and practitioners in all industries are at a point where they know there is a need to understand and use data more effectively to create result-based content, but the informational barriers to entry are often high.

For companies to succeed, they need to act fast and confident that the practical and strategic marketing content decisions they make, combined with the resource they deploy, are going to deliver end results faster and more frequently.

Data-driven Marketing Content, 1–10
Copyright © 2019 by Emerald Publishing Limited
All rights of reproduction in any form reserved
doi:10.1108/978-1-78973-817-920191002

This is where *Data-driven Marketing Content: A Practical Guide* helps.

This book explores the data-driven content opportunity, shares practical tips and expertise generated over thousands of business and marketing content projects and empowers you to make more successful content choices.

As you use this guide you will find chapter summaries, important term definitions and practical tips and advice, helping you to delve further into material that interests you the most, remove informational barriers sooner and digest information faster.

The Data-driven Content Process

The data-driven content process to follow when developing a repeatable system for marketing content creation that works can be effectively segmented into five stages:

(1) **Needs:** data discovery, opportunity and consolidating needs
(2) **Collection:** data collection, assessment and labelling
(3) **Processing:** data processing, storage and distribution
(4) **Management:** data managing, integrity and usefulness
(5) **Refinement:** data refinement, analysis and insights

Over the next few sections, we provide visualisations of this process in action, plus each segment previously referred to is discussed in greater detail.

Needs: Data Discovery, Opportunity and Consolidating Needs

The needs stage of the data-driven content process centres on the end user goals, objectives and desired outcomes from the data.

By putting clearly defined business data needs in place and matching these with solution-orientated outcomes and objectives, it becomes possible to outline expectations and describe practically what a successful data-led project looks like.

This 'needs phase' determines the attention of the collection stage.

Collection: Data Collection, Assessment and Labelling

Only once business data needs have been identified and agreed, can the collection stage begin.

Whilst it is likely you have a number of data discovery points in place already, it is necessary to take a step back from what's already present and contemplate what can potentially become available to fulfil your business data requirements. This provides a more comprehensive data collection body of work and expected improved foundation for future insights derived.

In most cases you will have silos of disparate business intelligence and data, which will require collecting into a single place. This assists you in the recombination of separate data points and sources for added and unique gains.

Once the data collection is at a required level of completion, you will need to review its accuracy, usefulness and compatibility for purpose. This can be a fairly succinct process and likely fairly subjective.

Practical Tip. As a quick tip, it is worth encouraging wider teams, staff and stakeholder involvement at this time. It is much easier to modify and add to data sets now rather than retrospectively.

When combining data sets and gathering information in a single database, you need to label everything. Labelling data is about making data meaningful and informative. Sharing suggested labels, and gathering wider team input through crowdsourcing feedback is critical for future usability and insights.

Processing: Data Processing, Storage and Distribution

As you may have noticed, the steps within the data-driven content process tend to overlap and integrate between phases.

The data processing phase considers the usefulness of the information derived from the data.

This functional step takes raw data and transforms them into processed information which is effectively stored for repeat use and distributed to the end users.

With each step of the process, you need to reflect on the successful application of the completed phase, re-evaluate whether it has delivered on all of the priority areas and needs identified then confirm this with stakeholders and end users.

You will want to limit assumed positive outcomes as much as possible while you progress to encourage data integrity later on.

Management: Data Managing, Integrity and Usefulness

Organising and managing your data is concerned with ensuring the data you have meet the current, changing and ongoing needs or your organisation.

Fundamental characteristics of this body of work include the ongoing maintenance of the data, the integrity of it and making sure it is fit for purpose.

Data management and assessed usefulness of work can often sit more effectively with key staff who are also end users of the data. This is primarily due to the fact that it will be their changing needs and outputs that are fundamentally dependant on the data usefulness.

Data integrity will usually be reliant upon the development and IT teams, accountable for data collection and processing; however, a feedback loop needs to be in place for any user to improve the value and usefulness from the data by reporting back to relevant departments: bugs, refinement, improvements and ideas.

The more that the wider company is included at the early stages of data-driven content, the easier it is to expedite the process and include these type of approaches within wider company departments and the business culture as a whole.

Refinement: Data Refinement, Analysis and Insights

The end goal of data refinement is the development of an integrated data source, which has successfully combined previous separate and dispersed data sets into a final product ready for new use.

Part of this stage involves creating commonality between the data points and the removal of vulnerabilities so that the data have a shared purpose and usefulness for gleaming fresh insight and analysis from.

It can be beneficial to consider this final part of the data-driven content process as an outcome, which refines data potential into information ready for analysis, insights and actions.

The Data-driven Content Process Chart

Fig. 1.1 gives you the visual representation of the data-driven content process in action.

Overcoming the Big Data Gulf

The quandary that this rapid influx of data is causing is that the super brands are able to invest heavily into turning these data into meaningful insight and immediate next actions; however, this is creating an ever-increasing gulf with the remaining 99% of businesses.

This big data gulf is no more present anywhere else than when it comes to creating effective business and marketing content that delivers on its objectives. The gap is more noticeable online, and this is reflected in this guide, but it is not exclusively so.

If you want to create digital marketing content that works, reflects the changing needs of your audience, and delivers results regardless of device and channel, **big data is the competitive advantage you are not yet maximising.**

It's important to mention at this time that data-driven content is not only about marketing content but also a changing approach towards creating any purposeful business content online or offline.

Big Data

Big data is a term most businesses and marketing professionals will have heard frequently over the past few years, with growing momentum and buzzword popularity since 2015. As you might expect, the term 'big data' can mean many things to various people; however, for the purposes of this book:

'Big data refers to large data sets that can be analysed, interrogated and processed in order to provide new meaning, value and understanding.'

Big data can be structured and unstructured, qualitative and quantitative, and is all encompassing.

A key characteristic to keep in mind with big data is the combination of 'high-volume' data accessibility and the potential to deliver increased data-driven advantages and insights (primarily to businesses).

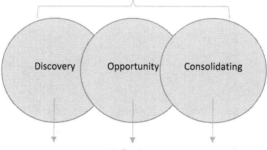

Needs:
The initial stage requires identifying, prioritising and setting/agreeing the business needs and focus areas.

Collection:
The second stage requires effective data gathering, confirmation of requirements and data qualification.

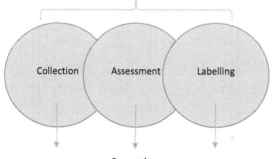

Processing:
Completing a series of operations on the data to make it more meaningful and ready for use.

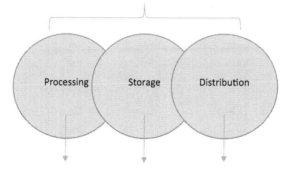

Fig. 1.1.   The Data-driven Content Process Chart.

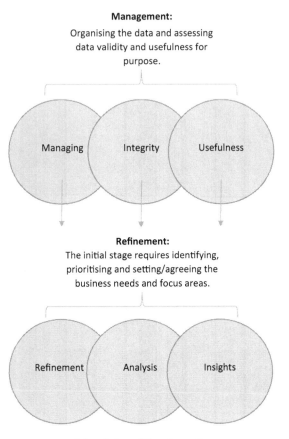

Fig. 1.1.   (Continued).

Another point to acknowledge is that big data is less about isolated quantities of data, rather an added focus on what you are able to do with the data to make better strategic and tactical decision-making.

The end goal being making more out of every piece of content you create, whether this is for marketing purposes or broader company needs.

The Fundamentals of Big Data

There are four fundamental characteristics to take note of with regard to big data, commonly referred to as 'The Four V's'.

You may find other sources citing 'value' as a fifth 'V', but this is a self-explanatory and an assumed feature, plus other reference points have been seen incorporating visualisation, viscosity and virality into the mix for other fundamental expansion.

The primary (Four V's) for big data which are described in greater depth next are:

(1) Volume
(2) Variety
(3) Velocity
(4) Veracity

More About the 'Four V's'

Volume can be seen as the fundamental criteria attributed to big data. Without scale you have data, but not the level of information required to derive any degree of competitive advantage or insight outside of the traditional informational expectations.

Variety is what makes big data all encompassing. There are thousands of mainstream data collation and access points (Google, Bing, YouTube, Google Analytics, Google Search Console, Facebook, Twitter, to name but a few); a visible characterisation of big data includes recombining these disparate data sets to support fresh (new) value. There are no rules with data variety, a Facebook feed, social media share, webinar, video transcript, and anything else you can think of, may have some level of data merit for future use.

Velocity refers to the rate and regularity of data requiring processing combined with the functionality of streaming that data. Modern televisions, computers, car sensors and any application or device that can send and receive data (consider the Internet of Things) contribute to velocity.

Veracity is the accuracy and trustworthiness of the data. You will have heard the saying 'garbage in, garbage out (GIGO)', this cannot be more overstated in importance when it comes to considering big data. If your data are not accurate or credible, everything you gather from them will be unreliable and flawed.

Business Insights and Value

Business insights (and ultimately actionable value) are the principal end goals for data driving any element of your business or marketing approach.

The building blocks and foundation for generating business insights and value are almost always people and technology. You should consider these two areas as the basis from which everything else is built upon.

The Business Insights and Value Stack

The Business Insights and Value Stack (Fig. 1.2) are something uniquely created for this guide. This stack comprises the five building blocks that are built (stacked) upon people and technology foundations.

The five stackable items are:

(1) **Data:** Needs, Collection, Processing, Management and Refinement
(2) **Information:** Knowledge and Presentation

Business Insights and Value

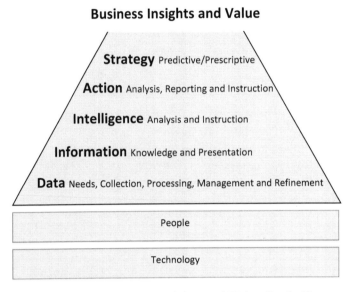

Fig. 1.2.   The Business Insights and Value Stack Chart.

(3) **Intelligence:** Analysis and Instruction
(4) **Action:** Analysis, Reporting and Instruction
(5) **Strategy:** Predictive/Prescriptive

Each of these stackable component parts build chronologically from the bottom upwards. Every step of the process is actively contributing towards the same objective area and end goal.

Data

We have covered the data item in some detail within 'The Data-driven Content Process' previously, including definitions for data needs, collection, processing, management and refinement.

For the contexts of this book, the term 'data' is chiefly represented as larger data sets and more specifically 'big data'.

As a reminder, big data refers to large data sets that can be analysed, interrogated and processed in order to provide new meaning, value and understanding.

Information

Data provided have a requirement to convey facts and details arranged and presented to encourage additional learning and logical understanding of the information contained.

Data visualisation impacts use, directs facts, and steers intelligence collected.

The knowledge component that is delivered signifies the progress made from data parameters and values on towards actual meaningful understanding for the user.

Intelligence

Intelligence develops from the prior knowledge state and represents the practical application of data-supported knowledge combined with end user skills.

The differentiator here is moving from awareness into actionable insights.

Action

The action phase is about empowerment to make something positive happen. In this circumstance, it relates directly to actionable analysis, reporting and instruction.

The data user can filter, recombine and manipulate the data for the purpose of unique insight, problem-solving and performance opportunity (plus analysis).

End users can create data-centric reporting, export data into other formats and use the intelligence as well as all information layers for benchmarking, reporting on success plus supplemental areas including forecasting.

The user is guided and directed towards actions as well as strategic decision-making.

Strategy

Strategy details how data can predictively and prescriptively assist with the expert/end user getting to the intended outcomes, goals and objectives.

Strategy is your plan to get to where you want or need to get to and often comprises a mixture of short-, medium- and long-term provisions and measurements for ensuring the business obtains and exceeds its overall goals.

Predictive and prescriptive evidence can be expedited through the provision of intelligent algorithms, Machine Learning (ML) and even Artificial Intelligence (AI), and whilst this may seem out of reach for the average business or practitioner, in fact all of these areas are much more attainable than they may first appear (which is discussed practically later in this business guide).

The chart demonstrates the stepping stone relationship and visual representation of The Business Insights and Value Stack in action.

Chapter Summary

In this opening chapter, you were introduced to the wealth of new data that is available to businesses and individuals, as well as the associated data dilemma this is causing. An initial opportunity that was covered reinforced that increased access to data also provides a vast untapped opportunity for those who are able to use it effectively.

This section of the guide discussed the fact that there is a growing gulf in marketing, and general content performance online, and highlighted the need for the majority of businesses (notably small- to medium-sized businesses) to become more effective in creating data-driven content in order to keep up with the super brands currently dominating and investing heavily into both data and content.

New approaches and ways of working were uncovered to help you see the broader picture and practical application of data-driven content (namely, 'The Data-Driven Content Process' and 'The Business Insights and Value Stack').

As you move into the next chapter, this guide delves into the data environment and understanding the key components that you need to be aware of including ML, AI, qualitative data and quantitative data.

At this point of the guide the dominant focus will move onto seeing the bigger picture, becoming aware of the main informational areas and gathering an understanding of the fundamentals of data-driven content, big data plus the wider ecosystem.

You will notice that, as you progress through this business guide, chapters will increasingly look at the practical aspects of creating marketing content that works and leveraging the potential that sits within your existing and new data for next levels of marketing gains.

Definitions

- Intelligent Algorithms: they are also referred to as artificial intelligent algorithms. This relates to computer systems that are able to replicate the logic, approach, expertise and reasoning behind processing information for problem-solving.
- Machine Learning (ML): a field of AI which relies upon statistical driven processes, functions and techniques to enable a computer to learn from new and changing data. It's the automated (self) learning without explicit programming that is core to ML.
- Artificial Intelligence (AI): AI, frequently coined machine intelligence, is the demonstration by computers (machines) to complete tasks normally associated to humans, traditionally requiring human involvement and intelligence. AI can cover many things such as problem-solving, learning from new data sets, as well as prescribing actions and meaning from new data.

Chapter 2

Understanding the Data Ecosystem

Whilst it may not appear to be the case, a form of data ecosystem has been around for thousands of years.

From early accounts of using data-driven insights to record and forecast crops and herds up to more refined accounting principles in the 1600s, which laid the basis of big data today, data ecosystems have played a fundamental part in many of the professional areas we experience in our everyday lives, and it is not new.

Something to consider as you progress through this chapter is that the data ecosystem is an ever-changing data-led collection of component parts (see Fig. 2.1) that are expected to develop and evolve over time.

It's for this reason this text refers to the data ecosystem as opposed to the data environment.

What Is a Data Ecosystem?

Simply put:

'A data ecosystem is a collection of component parts created with a single collective purpose – To produce meaningful insights from data.'

It is the usefulness and ever-evolving nature of data ecosystems that help to define them.

A data ecosystem can comprise a varied range of separate and contributing parts, plus one ecosystem can directly lead to the creation of another.

Typically, these (data ecosystems) will differ based on purpose; however, the frequent elements incorporated are detailed now.

Analytics – Platforms and programmes that support tracking, benchmarking, analysis, and reporting on data. This can be visualised as the front end and graphical user interface to the data presented to the end user in a logical, intuitive and user-friendly way. Analytics software packages and platforms support easy data use for search, filter and summary level information.

Infrastructure – Technical setup and collection of all related hardware, software, equipment, networks and facilities required during all stages of the data ecosystem. This will include processes, policies, data governance and standards, as well as data collection, management and associated functions.

Applications – Can be anything from Internet browsers and software like Skype through to sales management tools and mainstream Microsoft products for

Data-driven Marketing Content, 11–21
Copyright © 2019 by Emerald Publishing Limited
All rights of reproduction in any form reserved
doi:10.1108/978-1-78973-817-920191003

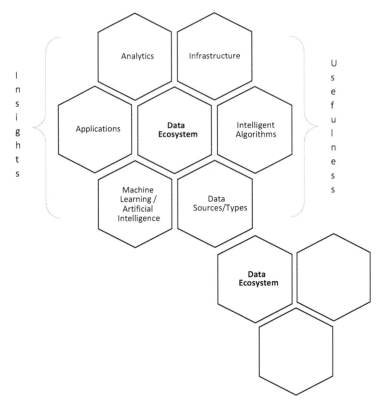

Fig. 2.1.   Building the Data Ecosystem Diagram.

business like Office, Word, Excel, PowerPoint and others. The application is any program or suite of programs designed for the end user to use the data effectively.

Intelligent Algorithms – Using the definition provided in Chapter 1, Intelligent Algorithms, also referred to as artificial intelligent algorithms, relate to computer systems that are able to replicate the logic, approach, expertise and reasoning behind processing information for problem-solving.

Machine Learning (ML) – ML is the field of Artificial Intelligence (AI) which uses statistical driven processes, functions and techniques to facilitate the ability for a computer (machine) to learn from new and changing data sets provided. It is the automated computerised (or 'self') learning without the prerequisite for explicit coding or computer programming that is the foundation of ML.

Artificial Intelligence (AI) – The demonstration by computers (machines) to fulfil the role and the actual completion of tasks which are usually classified as human actions and needing human intelligence.

Data Sources/Types – Data sources are fairly self-explanatory terminologies to describe the originating location or primary source of where the data came from.

This data source can range from Google documents and Excel spreadsheets to databases and forms. The data type is the characterisation of the data and normally defined by the values it holds, coding/programming languages used or the actions that can be used with the data types.

Machine Learning

At the time of writing this section of the guide, ML delivers over 6.76 billion results with a top-level Google UK search query, reinforcing the active interest in this field, as well as the confusion that often surrounds it.

What Is Machine Learning?

ML can mean many things to people, and common attempts to define it include the comments detailed below.

- The branch of AI that deals with systems and the ability for computers to learn from data and identify patterns without human intervention
- Practical application of AI, providing systems to automate actions and learn from changing data sets, improving the insights derived without any manual coding and programming involved
- The most basic practice of working with intelligent algorithms to process data, learn from the data, and make a judgement or prediction based on the data, providing new meaning and insights depending on data changes
- The science of enabling computers to act using data and make informed decisions attributed to the changing data they are exposed to

For the purposes of this guide, it's useful to consider ML as:

'Enabling computers to learn without extra coding or programming by reacting and adapting to the changing data sets it's exposed to.

The outcome of this learning is increased information and actionable insights from the data including prescriptive applications for real-world use.'

How Can Machines Truly Learn?

A computer is said to have the ability to learn based on increased exposure to data, longer time experience working with (and processing) data, tasked action progression and classification, in addition to the perceived value and performance of the computer for the tasks assigned. This is then combined with the review and assessment of any improvement made over time.

Machines can learn in a few ways, the most common learning types are discussed next, and the process in which machines learn can be seen in Fig. 2.2.

Supervised learning – Where the computer is given both the input and the expected output. Seen as a taught approach, the objective is for the computer (machine) to learn how to map specific inputs to the correct outputs.

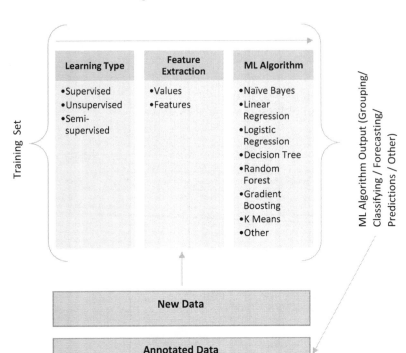

Fig. 2.2.   Machine Learning Process Diagram.

Unsupervised learning – Involves letting the computer figure things out on its own. For example, an objective with unsupervised learning can be for the machine to tell you something you didn't know about the data or to share patterns and opportunity that sit within the data.

Semi-supervised learning – Sitting between supervised and unsupervised learning, the computer is provided with partial information and training signals with the expectation that it will figure the remainder out for itself.

There are additional learning environments within the ML field including active learning and reinforced learning, but the above will give you enough of an understanding and awareness on the topic for the rationales of this guide.

If you are eager to dig deeper into the world of ML and the algorithm types involved, there are seven extra (commonly applied) algorithm-based models plus some top-level overviews to provide added awareness at this stage. These follow now.

Naïve Bayes (Classifier algorithm) – This is often deployed for grouping (or classifying) similar items together. Its uses include classifying documents, emails (think spam filtering) and wider applications including disease predictions and assigning sentiment to messages on platforms like Facebook.

Linear regression – It is a popular choice for businesses to make use of existing and historical data to predict the future. If your business wants to know how much stock to order based on seasonal change, linear regression can help. Other usual applications of this include estimating risk (for example, the cost of covering a person or business for insurance), as well as forecasting website traffic, sales and even staff recruitment.

Logistic regression – It is another classification of ML algorithm. If you want to assign a specific (discrete) value to data (yes/no, true/false, 0/1), this will enable you to accurately predict the probability. For example, an event business may want to know whether it will rain at a specific date range. Using this model and feeding in the relevant historical data will enable you to calculate the probability of raining. The same can be applied to any yes/no, true/false hypothesis as long as the data exist.

Decision tree – This is one of the most easy to understand and accessible examples of ML algorithms. Decision trees can be used for any series of events where the end result is currently unclear. An example that I like to use for this is helping a business to make a more accurate decision of whether to outsource a service (like PR, digital marketing, and other expert consultation areas) or bring the expertise in house. Decision trees can be classification-based or regression models.

Random forest – This is a similar approach to decision tree discussed previously but based on using a collection of decision trees (where the term 'forest' comes into play) to classify a new object based on the outcomes (or votes) for an end result. The uses can include the same as discussed in the decision tree information but where the data have gaps which get filled by the aggregation of decision tree votes. An example of this could be assessing the likelihood of a new bicycle tyre, getting a puncture by using the votes of the trees for a range of other similar products on the market.

Gradient boosting – This is typically used with decision trees in order to improve (boost) the quality of the outcome by improving the value of the base learner. Gradient boosting combines weaker predictors to provide more robust and higher prediction accuracy.

K means – This is a form of unsupervised (see previous sections) clustering ML algorithm that can classify and group data into any number of associated/ matched groups. An example of this in action includes visualising the scale of times a particular topic or term appears within your business website. If you have seen topical word cloud images in action (the bigger the word, the more the topic/ term is referenced within the data set), you have experienced a type of K means ML in action. Think about how the major search engines cluster related topics, words and information together based on the single search input you provide – this is K means and clustering ML.

How Can Machine Learning Be Used for Business?

The applications for ML for business purposes are too vast and varied to surmise in a single guide, and needless to say, ML have potential application to any business sector, brand, product or service areas.

Some of the more widely cited business uses of ML comprise everything from face detection and spam filtering in emails, all the way through to recommending songs, artists, films and television shows, plus the more B2B application of items such as speech recognition.

The sections that follow now cover practical ML applications applicable for many companies today.

Paid Advertising Automated Bid Adjustments and Insights
One area in which your business has probably experienced ML first hand will be in relation to Google and Bing paid advertising automated bid adjustment recommendations and real-time bidding through the respective bid management platforms.

By wading through the constantly changing data, ML algorithms provide information around user intent and search behaviour (among many other areas) and then prescribe bid changes and associated paid advertising campaign actions, to refine and improve your return on advertising spend or other objectives and goals set up within your accounts.

Predicting Future Sales Using Historical Data
A standard business challenge is effectively predicting growth. Whether you are looking to predict the impact of the weather or sales forecasting or the volume of footfall to your store tied to seasonal data (or realistically forecasting any metric (impressions, traffic, form completions, online transactions, etc.)), you can look to linear regression ML models (algorithms) to give you the solution.

At the point of sale, you can apply linear regression to forecast impact of your consultation services by looking back over your existing data sets and basing this for forward projections.

For any industry that can benefit from predicting the future by referring to the past (and what business would not want to do this?), ML can have a critical role and likely already is without you knowing it.

Artificial Intelligence

AI relates to a machine's (computers) capability to show intelligence as opposed to the natural intelligence demonstrated by human beings and other animals. As a facet of computer science, AI places emphasis on the creation of machines that can demonstrate intelligence and react/respond like humans.

Intelligence is related to intelligent agents and refers to any device that is able to take actions that increase the likelihood of achieving goals and objectives. Many of the same approaches for teaching AI are attributable to the teaching of children.

AI needs to be trained in structured and unstructured way (supervised, unsupervised, semi-supervised learning) and has to be exposed to different types of data sets (environments) and uses the lessons from these data sets to learn, adapt and improve (in the same way that people do).

Once AI becomes self-sufficient and able to understand the environment it operates within and the expected outcomes, it can tell us things we didn't already know or expect to discover through self-improvement.

It is this ability for AI to learn, problem-solve, and display qualities that represent the cognitive humanistic ability to adapt to a changing environment, which characterises AI.

To name but a few of the more common activities that AI are becoming known for, you would include solving complex problems; identifying patterns within huge data sets; recognising speech patterns, facial recognition, insight and opportunity identification, and even driving cars.

What Is the Purpose and Potential of Artificial Intelligence?

The potential for AI exists within every single aspect of life as it stands, plus everything new to follow. Businesses are already hugely invested in AI due to its commercial potential, and perhaps none more so than IBM at this time.

In the ongoing reinforcement for the growth and the role of AI technologies from IBM chairman, president and CEO Ginni Rometty, AI is seen as the all-encompassing computer-based fabric from which everything else will interact with and learn from.

From smart cities and self-driving logistics to medical diagnosis and treatment prescriptions, AI will be penetrating business independent of industry, expertise and tradition.

To go back to the question this section asked (what is the potential and purpose of AI?), the purpose of AI can be anything and everything. AI is not restricted to a single goal, event, or objective, it can be anything you want it to be and more than you ever imagined it could be.

To put this into meaningful data context, IBM chairman, Rometty, confirms that we are only using around 20% of the searchable data businesses have access to at the moment – 80% of these data are not generally being used.

How Can Businesses Use Artificial Intelligence?

We know and have reinforced that AI can be used for anything, plus contextualised the fact that AI can provide end results we never anticipated; however, there is an increasing wealth of practical applications of AI for business and a few of these are discussed here.

Search Engine Results Pages and Google RankBrain

Every business will have come into direct contact with ML and AI in practice, each time to search for information on the Internet.

Having worked in search engine optimisation (SEO) over many years a huge proportion of my working life has been directly impacted by understanding and optimising for ML systems and intelligent algorithms as a part of the wider AI (aka 'Google RankBrain').

On 25 October 2015, Google announced to the world the existence of Rank-Brain as a key component part of the Google Search Algorithm.

RankBrain relies on ML to inform its decisions on the relevancy (and therefore the ranking) of websites and other online entities by matching them to the most relevant search queries.

Google RankBrain serves billions of search queries daily spanning the globe and recombines many disperse data sets for the single purpose of delivering the best results as quickly as possible.

Some of the data points that Google RankBrain factors into its decision-making process include device used, location of the search, anticipated user intent, historical and changing search data and behaviour, changing trends related to the query, prior search activity of the user in question and broader personalisation criteria.

It is the ML capabilities for RankBrain to teach itself over some of the largest data sets imaginable which empower it to make increasingly accurate and effective 'guesses' (highly logical and almost always correct decisions driven by all of the available data) and emerging trends with the volumes of unique searches it experiences for the first time.

A solid proportion of daily searches have never been made before. Examples of this can be things like a football player changing teams, a new president being elected, new marketing campaigns, new technology and product understanding, new TV shows, theatre productions and music created plus never discovered, indexed or searched for previously.

Practically the AI element of Google RankBrain targets intent – What does the user really want to know? How can I provide them with the most relevant results to their query?

As an example of this RankBrain looks to understand what I want to see when I type or vocally search for any query like 'SEO'.

First what is my intent? I may want to know what SEO is, where to learn SEO, what companies sell SEO as a service, what are the best books or blogs to read about SEO, latest SEO industry events, etc.

Google RankBrain then factors in my past searches and personalised activities and will take a look at the device I'm using, and the type of results other people have engaged with on this same query.

It (RankBrain) will look at the broader range of most probable intention areas, consider the wider context of the query and provide me with a complete set of results (plus access to extra information seeking on the topic) so that I can either complete my intended end goal or easily refine my search more effectively by giving it more information to go on (after all a single term search like 'SEO' is not giving away much intent to go on).

'AI for Good'

As you would expect the notion of computers taking over the world is far more newsworthy and clickbait than the potential of AI to solve some of the world's biggest social and economic problems.

This is where 'AI for good' comes to the fore. This (AI for good) is a United Nations (UN) platform and growing movement where institutions are using AI to solve global issues like homelessness – in this example, AI is used to identify areas across the world where it predicts have the highest levels of homelessness to support added focus and support.

In this example, AI practically works by analysing satellite images and matching these to expected characteristics.

Qualitative Data

These are data that do not have a measurement for a specific attribute. As such qualitative data use approximations, interpretations and characterisations to describe something.

In this way you can describe qualitative data as data that are observed, categorised and recorded in a nonnumerical fashion.

Qualitative data are often gathered through focus groups, case studies, testimonials, interviews and other similar data collection approaches, giving researchers access to the meanings that people place onto things.

Examples of qualitative data in action include:

- Describing the taste of something
- Explaining how something looks
- Detailing a person's behaviour
- Summarising an event

Qualitative data can be great for gaining a more comprehensive understanding of how or why something happened, and getting extra insight into how people think and feel about any given situation.

The open-ended nature of qualitative data means that one set of findings can often act as the basis for a new phase of research, due to the expansive value that can be derived.

Disadvantages of qualitative data can include the more manual and laborious data collection requirements as well as the challenge for aggregating and normalising information for insights.

Quantitative Data

In direct contrast to qualitative data, quantitative data looks at the measurable (information about quantities) that can be categorised based on numerical values/ numbers alone – it does not look at the characteristics of the data, just the metric/ measurement.

Anything that has a number value assignable to it can be seen as quantitative data. Examples would include height, weight, clothing size, income amount, traffic volumes, number of sales and lots more.

Quantitative data examples include the following (note: these all have limited (closed) response types):

• Filling out a form
• Completing a survey
• Filing a government consensus

Chapter Summary

This chapter introduced the notion of the data ecosystem, how this differs from a data environment, plus the building blocks and visualisation of what a typical data ecosystem looks like (refer Fig. 2.1 for more information).

In this section, many of the key components that are active within data ecosystems were covered such as ML, AI, qualitative data and quantitative data, plus definitions spanning other related topics too.

This part of the business guide supplied insights into some of the practical applications of the broader theoretical areas including ML and AI, so that as a company these topics can start to be viewed with a more feasible mindset. This will help with furthering the thought process of how these areas can give your business a competitive advantage (something that will be targeted in a much greater extent throughout this guide).

As you move into the next chapter we take a look at extra real-world applications of big data for marketing and broader content creation. The guide considers how to collect data your business needs and ways to effectively manage your data, and highlights a few of the recent developments when it comes to data privacy/protection and particularly the role of GDPR.

Definitions

• Data ecosystems: these are expected to change, develop and evolve over time. A data ecosystem is a group of applications, analytics, technology and infrastructure used to collect, process and support big data.
• B2B: B2B, standing for business to business, is the acronym of the term used to describe companies that have a primary focus on selling to other businesses rather than directly to the consumer (B2C).
• Paid advertising: this relates to all types of business promotion and advertising which involves a direct payment. With paid advertising, companies are effectively paying for positions and advertising space rather than earning them (as you would with organic search). Paying for placement traditionally occurs within a bidding (or auction) environment.
• Automated bid adjustments: these are a form of paid advertising bidding strategy, often deployed on larger scale accounts, to enable more effective bulk bidding. Often these are based on setting parameters for bids tied to intended outcomes (for example, a targeted cost per acquisition).

- Search engine results pages (SERPs): these are the pages of information (organic and paid advertising along with integrated features like Google My Business and Google Answers) displayed in the search engines like Google, Bing, Duck-Duck-Go and others. SERPs display relevant results in a fast time (usually milliseconds) tied to any given search query.
- Google RankBrain: this is the AI and ML algorithm and name the search engine provider Google use for understanding new and niche search queries.

Chapter 3

Data Collection and Management

The previous two chapters in this data-driven marketing content guide have been predominantly informational and theoretical, introducing some concepts that may be completely new to you and reinforcing the key component parts that enable businesses to realise the potential from big data for creating a competitive business advantage.

In this chapter, we explore the practical data points and resources that your organisation can gather and manage, and analyse important data points to drive your content creation process.

This section provides a framework for managing your data and summarises a few of the changing industry requirements for business with consideration of General Data Protection Regulation (GDPR) and the role that it plays in marketing content.

Data Collection Points

Let's start with a few pertinent data questions:

- How much of the entire data universe that is relevant to your business do you currently have access to?
- Can you make quick and easy business decisions from your data?
- Is your data accurate, meaningful and fit for purpose?
- Do you have hypothesis that you cannot answer with the data you have?

It is these and other fundamental data questions which this section of the guide answers in a practical way.

Data Collection

Data collection, integrity and management underpin every aspect of business decision-making. It is the foundation for meaningful professional choices and the leading indicator for marketing content ideation, delivery and refinement.

If you are like many professionals, practitioners and business teams, you will generate and have access to all types of data, information points, as well as internal resources.

Data-driven Marketing Content, 23–49
Copyright © 2019 by Emerald Publishing Limited
doi:10.1108/978-1-78973-817-920191004

In many cases, data points will be disparate, segmented and difficult to combine for broader insights and content actions outside of the parameters from which the data sets were derived. In fact, this tends to be the business norm.

Each of these separate data points will fulfil a basic business need (for example, 'how many calls have the sales team made this day/week/month?'), a degree of trend awareness, plus basic comparative abilities (for example, 'how does these days/weeks/months sales calls compare with the same timeframe last year?').

An important part of effective data collection is the increased efficiency and effectiveness of recombining data from numerous sources to develop extra and new meaning, insights and ultimately business value, competitive advantage and performance improvements.

Data Collection for Marketing Content Creation

There is a wealth of data available for free and through paid subscriptions to business.

In fact, some of the largest business dilemmas faced today include being able to identify the data sources they need, reducing the amount of time taken to get information and insights from the available data and prioritising the items to implement (whilst managing the data, reviewing its integrity, keeping momentum with actionable backlogs and other factors too).

Since the early 2000s, I've been leading digital, marketing, IT and content teams; worked with hundreds of data sources and led thousands of data-driven content campaigns.

In this section of the marketing content guide, I share some of the most useful data points (sources of data) that will empower your business to collect the data needed to progress your companies content creation to a greater level of opportunity identification, performance and results against your objectives.

Content Building Data Sources (Points) for Business

There are a myriad of free and paid for (subscription based) data points, tools and analytical software packages for companies to consider. Listed below are a number of those that are most suitable for data-driven content creation.

You will also find in this part of the guide, a practical decision tree approach to assist you with deciding on the future tools and data points you will be reviewing for future business requirements (see Fig. 3.1).

Analytics Tools and Data Sources

Google

There is a growing quantity of free and paid for options when it comes to the varying array of tools that Google provide for business. To see a list of all of them, you can navigate to https://www.google.co.uk/about/products/ using any web browser.

You will often find that Google and other tools, data and analytics providers provide standard use access to data from free and subscription alternatives.

In my experience, the subscription options in most cases are for the enterprise level, large brand organisation, outside of the vast majority of other business needs. Also, restrictions are frequently data sample size based (including the case of Google Analytics (GA)) as opposed to core feature provisions, meaning that any impact is negligible if any.

As an example of this in action, GA provides its 360 version as well as the standard GA free version.

Google products are divided into three categories:

(1) For all
(2) For business
(3) For developers

As a company, practitioner or delivery team with data-driven aspirations, it's useful to have awareness of all of them.

Google Products 'for All'
Here is the list of the products listed within the Google tools and products for everyone (or all) at the time of writing this guide. It is worth investing some time reviewing these when you can as you will likely have bespoke company needs that these can help with outside of the scope of this data-driven marketing content remit.

You will see highlighted (bolded) below the items which are covered in more detail.

(1) Android Auto
(2) Android Messages
(3) Android OS
(4) Calendar
(5) Cardboard
(6) Chrome
(7) Chrome Web Store
(8) Chromebook
(9) Chromecast
(10) Connected Home
(11) Contacts
(12) Daydream View
(13) Docs
(14) Drawings
(15) Drive

(16) Earth
(17) Finance
(18) Forms
(19) Gboard
(20) Gmail
(21) **Google Alerts**
(22) Google Allo
(23) Google Cast
(24) Google Classroom
(25) Google Cloud Print
(26) Google Duo
(27) Google Expeditions
(28) Google Express
(29) Google Fit
(30) Google Flights
(31) Google Fonts
(32) Google Groups
(33) Google Input Tools
(34) Google One
(35) Google Pay
(36) Google Play
(37) Google Play Books
(38) Google Play Games
(39) Google Play Movies & TV
(40) Google Play Music
(41) Google Store
(42) Google Street View
(43) Google Wifi
(44) Google for Education
(45) Google+
(46) Hangouts
(47) Inbox by Gmail
(48) Keep
(49) Maps
(50) News
(51) Photos
(52) Pixel 3
(53) Play Protect
(54) Project Fi
(55) Scholar
(56) Search
(57) Sheets
(58) Sites
(59) Slides
(60) Tilt Brush
(61) Translate

(62) Trips
(63) Voice
(64) Waze
(65) Wear OS by Google
(66) **YouTube**
(67) YouTube Gaming
(68) YouTube Kids
(69) YouTube Music
(70) YouTube TV
(71) Zagat

Google Alerts. By creating Google alerts and notification updates, you are able to receive email updates based on any brand, site, product, service, trend or topical indexed search result.

You can gather fresh data and information to create news items; blog posts; and latest trends, exhibitions and events pertinent to your industry and business.

You can get creative with Google alerts and monitor change detection on competitor sites and broader industry movements, granting your company pro-active and changing access to information tailored for you.

Practical Tip. To create a Google alert:

- Go to https://www.google.com/alerts
- Enter the search query/term/topic
- Click 'show options' to specify your settings
- Click 'create alert'

You can manage your alerts anytime: edit, create and delete as appropriate.

YouTube. YouTube, the second largest search engine (Google being the first), features heavily within most Google search engine results pages (SERPs), having been bought out by Google in November 2006.

Referencing Omnicore Agency 2018 publicly accessible YouTube statistics (see reading references at the end of this guide), YouTube has:

- 1.9 billion active monthly users and 30+ million daily active users
- 300,000 paying YouTube TV subscribers
- Over 5 billion video shares to date
- 50 million users creating content
- 5 billion videos watched per day

Bringing this back to business data for marketing content creation, YouTube analytics (https://studio.youtube.com) supplies analytical information related to your YouTube channel spanning:

- Watch time
- Views and unique views

- Subscribers
- Reach
- Traffic sources
- Impressions click through rate
- Demographics (language, age, gender, countries and more)

Practical Tip. By reviewing the data in your YouTube analytics account (this is a free analytics account), you can create video marketing content that reflects the audience demographics and refine videos to echo the sentiment within the data on metrics like watch time to produce video content that works harder for you.

You are able to test and apply a continuous improvement methodology by trialling video titles, descriptions, destination targeting and more – all with data freely available within your account.

Google Products 'for Business'
Below is the list of the products detailed in the Google tools and products 'for business'. You will see in bold the items which are covered in more detail and have greater relevancy to data-driven marketing content data sources.

(1) AdMob
(2) AdSense
(3) AdWords Express
(4) **Analytics**
(5) Android
(6) Assistant
(7) Blogger
(8) Chrome
(9) Data Studio
(10) DoubleClick by Google
(11) G Suite
(12) **Google Ads**
(13) Google Certified Shops
(14) Google Cloud Platform
(15) Google Domains
(16) Google Enterprise Search
(17) Google Manufacturer Center
(18) Google Maps APIs
(19) Google Merchant Center
(20) **Google My Business**
(21) Google Shopping Campaigns
(22) Google Surveys
(23) Google Tag Manager
(24) **Google Trends**
(25) Google Web Designer
(26) Google+ Brands

(27) Hire
(28) Local Inventory Ads
(29) **Optimize**
(30) **Search Console**
(31) The Digital Garage
(32) Waze Local

Over the next few pages, I provide substantial focus on free Google tools and software packages as well as the myriad of other free data points and sources that I have applied and real-world experience working with over many years.

If you are looking for practical tips and advice, plus new data-led ideas, these sections will prove extremely useful.

Analytics (Google). GA is a free (and 360 alternative, a paid for) tool which I would urge every website owner to take full advantage of and combine GA insights and data with those of Google Search Console (GSC), as they are a perfect data marriage. Note: there is more on GSC later in this section.

GA enables people to get a more complete data picture and deeper under-standing of their customers so that all of these data can be used to improve the customer experience, refine and target people more effectively and increase your results, revenue and digital return on investment (ROI).

In the context of data-driven marketing content, GA empowers businesses to identify and prioritise the right kind of content their audience wants and needs and turns a potentially good idea into a functional and effective content output that works towards your objectives.

GA removes a lot of the informational barriers between people regardless of role, experience and levels of data expertise to do the following:

- Identify content that delivers traffic, revenue and goal completions
- See and compare types of marketing content that is engaged with more and actively shared
- Gather insights on content gaps including those driven by users searching the site
- Generate and customise reports that reflect business goals and objectives
- Access machine learning algorithms and actionable insights without any expertise required
- Understand how other marketing channels are interacting, assisting conver-sions and contributing towards total website performance and success
- Review trend changes, opportunities and both internal and external potential influences
- Collaborate, share and use data within and from exporting out of GA, regardless of your needs

Practical Tip. GA provides you with all of the post-click data, plus some leading indicators including keywords used (not all, but GSC helps a great amount with that piece), traffic sources, user demographics and everything you initially need to create some meaningful data-led content.

Narrowing down GA to a couple of tips is almost impossible, so here are some of my most frequently deployed tactics that I refer to when creating new marketing content using this tool (analytics package).

Firstly, GA helps me with removing question marks and answering content questions I have as a digital marketing expert, such as:

- What content drives the most traffic, sales, pageviews, engagements, social shares?
- Is my marketing content performing better/worse than last year/month/week/day?
- What content are people searching for on my site? Does it exist? Should it?
- Which pages are underperforming? How can I improve them?
- What quick opportunities/wins are available to give my content a performance boost?
- Does my marketing content work and deliver results on mobile devices, tablets and desktops?
- Where are most of my visitors coming from? What are they interested in? How can I make refinements to target them more effectively?
- Where are people exiting the site? What content are they seeing? How can I get them to progress through the buying cycle and stop them bouncing (exiting the site without having any interactions, clicks or other engagements)?

Common actions I may look to complete specific to data-based marketing content creation include the following items.

Revisiting old content to make it work harder. Blogs and news sections of websites are fantastic for shorter term impressions and traffic; however, the value they bring doesn't have to end there. By logging into GA and going to 'Behaviour > Site Content > All Pages', you can see the top performing pages on your site by a myriad of metrics (including traffic and pageviews) and use this to discover the top performers over any timeframe.

You can then use this data to choose topics to revisit pages, to add fresh marketing content to (insights, opinions, statistics and more) and turn limited time performing content into longer term, repeat contribution content cornerstones (also referred to as hero content and evergreen content).

Discovering underperforming content. Looking at year on year (YoY) performance of pages in GA (go back to 'Behaviour > Site Content > All Pages' and set the date range filter option 'compare to' and set 'previous year') means that you can find out why certain pages, topics and products are not delivering the gains they have done previously. I use this type of fast fact-finding to trigger new actions and content updates.

Things I would check to decide what actions I would take include the following:

- External ranking marketing content (SWOT analysis)
- Google trends and changing search behaviour

- Internal page/content metrics: bounce rates, session duration, engagement levels, latest content updates
- External content metrics: social shares, backlinks, comments

I could then create an action plan and refine the marketing content accordingly.

Identify which content leads towards sales and goal completions. By going into 'Behaviour > Behaviour flow' in GA, you have direct access to the interactions people are making to visualise how they navigate and move around your site.

With this information you can identify and impact (positively improve) the following:

- Pages where people are dropping out of your sales funnel
- Supporting pages people view prior to converting
- The number of pages/interactions people typically need to buy (and therefore the opportunity to reduce this for quicker and more effective sales journeys)

Reveal the types of content your audience like the most. And create more of it. From video content and infographics to listicles, surveys and deep content articles, the more you know about your audience wants and needs, the easier it becomes to match them with fantastic marketing content.

For this task, I like to prioritise marketing content that lands people onto the site for the first time and drives them to return. In GA, I would then click 'Behaviour > Site Content > Landing Pages', but you could look at all traffic instead (by going to 'Behaviour > Site Content > All Pages').

Act on data to encourage more people to return. Returning visitor metrics are regularly an overlooked expert attention area because so much time, money and resource is placed on getting more new users to people's websites. A return visitor is already in your buying cycle, they will convert sooner and act faster (whether this is a video engagement, form completion, telephone call or sale, they are closer to converting).

To see what your returning visitors are doing, how their behaviour differs to new site visitors and therefore give them more of what they need to encourage more people returning to the site, go to 'Audience > Behaviour > New vs Returning'.

Google Ads. The paid advertising platform and associated data insights and analytics package associated to advertisements, offerings, product listings, video content and mobile app installs within the Google advertising network (https://ads.google.com).

The benefits of Google Ads (previously Google Adwords) includes finding out the following:

- How your business is being found spanning the paid web including data on ads for: search, display, video and apps

- Your reach to your potential and actual audience, whether this is in terms of the immediate local and a handful of mile, or regional, national and global data
- People and advert targeting – ad frequencies, coverage, website clicks, calls and a lot more
- Advertising budget and direct advert testing, refinement and management

Google My Business. Accessible from https://www.google.com/business/, Google My Business (GMB) gives you access to data about how people are searching for, interacting with, and finding your business/brand and offices/stores/locations within Google Search.

Data provided through GMB includes views, calls, clicks and other GMB engagements, plus downloadable data which you can repurpose and recombine with other data sets for new use.

You can use GMB to find out where your customers are coming from; how many of them are requesting directions to your stores and what content, photos, videos and other media are generating interest with your target audience.

Practical Tip. The GMB 'Post' feature, is something introduced in 2018 and lets you publish marketing content, events, discounts, promotions and more directly into the GMB search feature within the Google search itself.

This type of ongoing content and brand promotion within the SERPs helps businesses to take up a greater proportion of the potential SERP retail space for all search queries in which the organic GMB-rich feature/listing appears for.

Gains from added GMB retail space coverage vary including pushing down the related search 'People also search for' widget that generally includes competitors into lower CTR (click through rate) parts of the page and making existing marketing content and promotions work harder – for free!

Google Trends. You can get to Google Trends from any web browser by copying/pasting the following into the address bar (https://trends.google.com/trends/).

The Google Trends site presents access to analysis from Google on the top search queries spanning the globe, incorporating numerous regions and languages, with the purpose of comparing, tracking and acting on timeline (trends) data over time.

The opening dashboard of insights from Google Trends provides latest stories and insights, trending topics and events, seasonal changes, yearly aggregate search trends, plus new Google initiatives and associated news.

Practical Tip. Use Google Trends in combination with other tools like Google Keyword Planner, GSC, GA, plus your own hypothesis and industry-related expertise as another layer of data-led justification and insights.

If I am a marketing expert looking to create new business content on a specific topic area, I want to make sure that the terminology used is reflective of growing and current trends, rather than declining search behaviour – Google Trends is perfect for that.

As a company, you may be wanting to narrow down advert headline options or looking to create content to piggyback off new, latest and changing media trends and industry interest areas. You can support any Google Alerts and notifications (see earlier coverage on this topic) and combine this with Google Trends insights for increased actionable insights.

By completing this recombination of separate data sets, you are able to look to create fresh insights that will help with the pitching of content, refinement for existing marketing content (tied to headline and title changes), as well as the creation of new content that you can be confident has an active demand for.

It is much easier to commit time, resource and money to developing new content when you can be confident it has a greater opportunity to perform and deliver upon energies invested and ROI.

Optimize (Google). Google Optimize (GO) is already integrated within GA and works in partnership with GA data by letting you act on data insights to directly experiment and test hypothesis.

GO can be used to A/B, split and multivariant test pretty much anything and the best bit is that you do not need to have website development or design skills to use it. Thanks to the fact that there is a 'what you see is what you get' (WYSIWYG) graphical user interface, which lets to click and set changes.

A huge part of effective marketing content is the ongoing testing, updates, tweaks, and refinement process – all of which you can complete using GO.

Practical Tip. Put together a shared Google doc or Excel file and ensure that all the key stakeholders have access to this and can populate it with things they would like to test along with supporting data including the priority of the suggestion and the anticipated impact.

It's important to make the experiments (things people want to test) as specific and granular as possible, as often it will be different people implementing the updates in GO.

Examples of GO experiments can include the following:

- Changing the wording on a button (for example, from 'more details' to 'continue')
- Adding in new calls to action (CTAs)
- Moving short forms for conversion rate optimisation (CRO)
- Changing main headings (h1 tags)
- Adding new sub headings
- Changing/adding new images

Search Console (Google). Formerly Google Webmaster Tools, GSC, is the first port of call for all your pre-click (you may recall GA being the post-click equivalent to GSC) data and analytics business needs.

At the time of writing this article, two versions of GSC are available for business; the historical version which you can get to from https://www.google.-com/webmasters/tools and the new version which will replace the previous version completely at some point once all features are transferred and other testing is complete.

You can access the new version of GSC at https://search.google.com/search-console.

I would recommend using both of the available versions of GSC for as long as they are openly accessible as they do offer different data insights and nuances for quick data content wins.

Practical Tip. If there was only one tool that can be used for new marketing content ideas and writing content from the available data, I would recommend GSC. Obviously, businesses do not need to make this choice, but I hope this reinforces the value that GSC can bring to your future content efforts when GSC is used to its full potential.

There are many fast and basic actions that provide repeatable marketing content wins when digging into GSC data, a few of my favourite ones are listed next.

High Opportunity Existing Page Updates and New Content Identification

When you filter performance data by high impressions and low clicks, you have direct access to the search terms that offer you business with the greatest traffic potential related to your current search visibility.

The low current click supporting metric enables you to look for the biggest disparities (high impressions low clicks) and group these terms into closely related topics and content titles for mixed content building (zero click, high impression terms groups are perfect for new marketing content gap identification and fulfilment).

As an example of this in action, you may see that you are generating a total of 15,000 impressions for terms that include the phrase (note: GSC has easy filter options) 'new business'. From this, you can set top impression terms (those likely to be two- to three-word phrases), medium impact terms and longer tail queries (four to six words plus).

By adding in the filter metrics for position and CTR in GSC, you can then match terms and opportunity to existing content and enhance the content claim, authority and relevance to these groups of terms.

Typically, actions to make your current marketing content improve would include the following:

- Title tag updates (a ranking factor) and more importantly relevancy signal offering CTR support within the search results, as this is the prominent advert heading for Organic Search
- On page content updates, core term seeding and refinements to headings (header tags h1–h6), introductory paragraphs that theme the page, and natural variations within the main body text
- Content expansion – FAQs are great for this, as are related reading and definition segments. This is about removing informational barriers for the user and extending the content breadth and depth of coverage with expected terms seen on high-quality articles

- Technical updates to help search engines understand and rank the content; things like adding video transcripts and updating image files names and alt text
- Internal linking with relevant anchor (link) text, helping users navigate within text reading to other topical pages on the site and support the website's internal trust signals to the topic area

Then you can create the types of marketing content that most successfully service the user intent on the topic on their needs. It's important to look at the top-ranking content as well as the search verticals present.

For the topic 'new business', this may result in new content for the following:

- Guides
- Video
- Google Rich Result targeted content
- Blog post
- News article
- FAQs for service landing pages
- Other

Answer-based Content Driven by Your Audience

When filtering by performance > queries in GSC and selecting 'filter by query' you can apply any filter term parameter to narrow down the data you see. Using questions like who, what, why, where, when, how as well as other comparison and buyer intent queries including compare, best, cost, price, and more, you can very quickly see what the spectrum of needs are for your audience associated to your website.

Even without any existing FAQ content on your site, it is likely that the service, product and industry relevancy will enable your site to be associated to these groups of questions and therefore be shown (visible) to them. This means that your GSC account will be capturing some of this potential opportunity and allow you to prioritise marketing content creation to support it.

If you do not have any visibility or association to question and answer (FAQ) type content, you can take the initial steps by adding known (speak to first line staff, sales people, and delivery teams) questions and common barriers people have towards converting to core business pages, as well as creating a dedicated FAQ resource and definitions/glossary page.

These types of new visibility starting points will enable your business to grow and expand based on data justifications.

Connecting Google Search Console to Google Analytics for Added Data Insights

The easier it is to share data between analytics packages, the deeper the data-driven insights become and the faster it is to access the value from it.

Once you have a site verified in GSC and GA, you can quickly enable GSC data within GA through the Admin > (navigate to the relevant search console property) > Property settings > Save.

After GA removed a large proportion (often approximately 80%) of the keywords data from its interface, the ability to bring in GSC data and counter some if this impact, plus add extra data insights, can be a meaningful exercise for easy data changes.

Building Linkable and Likeable Marketing Content

GSC (via 'links' in the main navigation area) tells you the top external linking websites, the external link details on a page by page basis, plus the top linking text people are using to point referring backlinks to your marketing content.

With this information you can identify link gaps, see what content is driving link activity, and create new content to either fuel more of the same intent link building, and fill gaps within the core authority areas of your business and website.

Google Products 'for Developers'

Here's the developer centric list of the products detailed in the Google tools and products 'for developers'. These have been included for completeness of coverage as, for the purposes of this chapter, there is no requirement to drill into these further as they have by nature very distinct purposes outside the scope of this guide.

(1) App Testing
(2) Cloud Computing
(3) Devices
(4) Engagement
(5) Game Services
(6) Growth
(7) Maps + Location
(8) Messaging + Notifications
(9) Monetisation
(10) Monitoring
(11) Payments
(12) Sign in + Identity
(13) Storage + Sync

Free Content Tools

So far the focus for analytical tools and data sources has been Google, a deliberate choice based on the direct potential value that tools like GA, GSC, GO and others provide and warrant extra coverage in this section of the guide.

Now we move on to a broader set of free tools and analytics software, along with some of my top practical uses, tips and advice for your future marketing content projects.

I want to reinforce at this stage that I do not have any affiliations to these products or solutions; however, I have lots of experience using them successfully for various content campaigns, in some cases over many years.

What follows are my top free tools which will supercharge your content creation by providing you with new data and associated content insights within a matter of seconds.

The focus here has been on 'free' over paid tools, and this is based on the variety and value which you can derive from freely available software and perfectly applicable alternatives to a few of the mainstream paid for versions.

The content tools provided include a wealth of practical application areas, meaning that once you have finished this chapter you will be able to directly apply these tools into your approach for data fed content development.

Answer the Public for content ideas

Available through your web browser at https://answerthepublic.com/, Answer the Public has a 'Go Pro' version, but in all my time using this tool for quick content ideation based on questions, answers and related topical information, I have never needed to upgrade.

To use this tool you simply add a word or a phrase to the 'get ideas' search bar and within a matter of seconds you will have data related to the top, semantically relevant terms/phrases/data for the following:

- Questions
- Prepositions
- Comparisons
- Alphabetical
- Related

Practical Tip. By using sources like this intermittently, you can fill gaps in your content marketing calendar and ensure that the content you are creating reflects the audience behaviour and needs.

Every relevant question is a potential blog post or FAQ item. Common themes can become hero/cornerstone/evergreen content, offering deeper showcasing of expertise, authority and trust (EAT), a key ranking factor and part of the added emphasis within the 'Google Raters Guidelines'.

As an example of this tool in action, I added the term 'SEO' and outputs included:

Questions

'are'
are seo and sem the same thing
are seo tools worth it
are seo keywords important

are seo companies worth the money
seo are meta tags important
what are seo backlinks
what are seo best practices
what are seo techniques
'where'
where seo is used
where to learn seo
where to put seo keywords in html
where to find seo clients

Prepositions

'for'
seo for wordpress site
seo for shopify store
seo for youtube
seo forums
seo for small business
seo for amazon

And Comparisons (To Name a Few of the Immediate Data Examples Given)

'vs'
seo vs traditional marketing
seo vs paid search
seo vs content marketing

As an extra tip, if you just want to take out any of the time it takes to create a blog post and choose from the many options that Answer the Public supplies, you can use a free HubSpot tool (https://www.hubspot.com/blog-topic-generator) which gives you five example blog titles driven by any keyword you choose (there is a paid for upgrade too, but for the quick and dirty 'give me some blog titles' requirements the free one works a treat).

Site:search competitor content creation

By using search operators within the Google search engine results pages, you get access to the indexed and ranked content on any website, plus you can refine this down to any interest area.

This means that you can type in a competitor URL, or high-ranking site, and compare the content they have to your website, identify gaps, marketing content types, and reverse engineer this for your business (ideally factoring in content improvements too).

Practical Tip. To use this functionality, you type into Google site:example-website – so for Wikipedia, this would be site:wikipedia.org.

Following the site:wikipedia.org through, there are 148 million indexed pages from the all site data. This is too much to work with so I will refine it to a topic, in this case 'dogs'.

I do this with the following query – site:wikipedia.org "dogs".

This narrows my content opportunity discovery to a refined 187,000 pages.

I only really want to know about pages dedicated to dogs, so I look at URLs containing the word 'dog' (I removed the pleural as 'dog' will incorporate this): site:wikipedia.org inurl:dog now gives me 3,320 results – we are getting there.

One final refinement will give me a manageable volume which is broad enough to ensure I'm not missing out on content ideas:

By appending 'breed' to my previous search operator I now only see 483 pages which have 'dog' in the URL and reference 'breed' within the content.

My final query (which you can change to anything relevant to your content searches) is: site:wikipedia.org inurl:dog "breed".

As a bonus tip, you can quickly copy/paste all the search results into an Excel file including the advert content by using a free tool/Chrome browser extension called LinkClump, otherwise you can select all and manually copy/paste; however, the manual approach will require formatting and take a little more of your time to do.

Alchemy Text for understanding intent

If you are aware of great examples of external marketing content or have created content but want to use natural language processing machine learning to understand how the content comes over in regard to intent, emotion, keywords and more, then https://natural-language-understanding-demo.ng.blue mix.net/ can be a useful free content creation and understanding data point for you.

Practical Tip. Tools like this are perfect for identifying existing user intent and re-pitching existing content to fulfil the audience needs and wants.

I love to make the most out of existing content wherever possible, and this free tool is a great way to evaluate and target intent from historical content which either did not have intent targeting in place when the content was originally created or the purpose of the marketing content has changed since its initial inception.

You can also act on competitor intent content marketing and factor into your marketing calendar any audience intent gaps (think in terms of informational, educational, transactional, locational types of intent).

Choosing the best keywords with Ubersuggest

Provided for free by ex Googler Neil Patel (at https://neilpatel.com/ubersuggest/), Ubersuggest pulls in keyword data to give you the following:

- Increased data on the term and related terms (trends, seasonality, cost per clicks)
- Keyword suggestions to help expand the content coverage and perceived quality and reach of your piece being created
- SERP ranking details for examples of the ranking content to beat/better in your posts
- Keyword difficulties and related information to help decide the likelihood of ranking tied to the competitive nature of the terms targeted

Whilst all content creation is not about ranking in Google, the data insights like those listed previously are important for understanding demand, competing sites and related areas important for content justification and increased changes of performance against objectives.

Curating content from audience feedback

Through Quora (https://www.quora.com/) you are able to interact and engage with audiences and influencers by asking and answering questions.

Quora is a useful and highly underutilised (although it's growing fast) question and answer forum-based social platform which includes some of the biggest names and personalities spanning lots of industries.

Quora can be used for sourcing quotes, opinions and insights as part of existing and fresh content updates, as well as a platform for sharing expertise and promoting insights from content you have already built.

Obvious uses of Quora include new content discovery based on trends and active topic areas driven by data on the types of questions people are asking and the volume of interaction, sharing and commenting taking place.

Practical Tip. I like to use Quora for gathering qualitative data, quotes and open-ended survey information for building new marketing content and ensuring the content created matches user terms and variations.

Unique data-based content helps the shareability and natural performance on website content as it gives you something new to say, opportunity for showcasing opinion, plus imbedded quotes, insights and snippets that are useful for ego bait content promotion and linking.

Once proficient with Quora, you may opt to delve into Reddit (https://www.reddit.com/); however, whilst it is great for social listening and trend identification, be cautious when it comes to any self-promotion, as Reddit users tend to have little patience when it comes to clear brand misuse of the platform (and in many cases this is why Reddit has such an active and engaged audience and is able to deliver genuine audience insights).

Linkbait title generator to create headlines that work

A lot of focus has been on free content tools that help you find new content ideas, see the bigger picture and use the terms and intent suitable to your audience.

Now it is time to entice the user to click on your content (whether paid, organic or other media including emails and newsletters). This is where the heading becomes so important.

Linkbait Title Generator (available at https://www.contentrow.com/tools/link-bait-title-generator/) helps with refining titles and expanding the titles to consider as part of your content brainstorming sessions, with the application of clickbait terms and emotive keywords, to suggest topic and title-based query variations.

For example, by adding the query 'data drive content', I am provided with Linkbait titles including the below:

- 9 reasons you can blame the recession on data-driven content
- 13 amazing facts about data-driven content

Practical Tip. Use GA and GSC to identify existing marketing content on your website which ranks well, receives high impression levels, but is not delivering the traffic levels (lower CTR) expected.

Update the title tag and the main h1 tag/heading on the content. Annotate GA with the date the changes are made and revisit the data 2–3 weeks later once you have a large enough data set to review.

I would expect to see increased CTR and therefore traffic to the updated posts. If not, test another heading/title tag variation and continue to do this until you are satisfied that the traffic is in line with the sites average CTR, and/or optimised effectively.

This type of CTR optimisation on historical content should be part of your data boosting activities most, if not all, months.

Staying 'in the Know' with Feedly RSS

The main use of Feedly (https://feedly.com/) for content is the awareness of new sources of data (stats and other content includers), plus stories (blogs, videos, news, other) that you can use for newsjacking and demonstrating business expertise through new volumes of trending industry/service/product interest.

Feedly pulls in data from many separate sources and gives you personalised setting-based updates when and how you want them.

If your business operates within a highly changeable industry, or you are eager to be seen as a key thought leader and influencer in your market, fats reaction times to latest content trends can form a genuine differentiator.

Paid Content Tools

Almost every free tool you can get access to has some form of paid alternative; but in my experience, a vast majority of the data sources and tools I use for business purposes are free – this is reflected by the imbalance between the free tools I've shared previously in this guide and the paid tools I share below.

I should also state at this point that Apollo Insights platform (more on this here – https://www.vertical-leap.uk/apollo-insights/) is my go to prescriptive marketing platform for pretty much all my SEO and search marketing first ports of call in my role as Head of SEO.

I haven't covered this (Apollo Insights) in more detail as I am directly affiliated to the company and wanted to provide minimum bias in this guide.

BuzzSumo for analysing and producing content fit for social media and backlink building

There is a free version of BuzzSumo (see https://app.buzzsumo.com/research/content), but it has many other features and deeper data trends that are only accessible through the paid version, hence its inclusion in the paid content tools section.

The free version of BuzzSumo is perfect for quick data insights into latest trends by topic and external performance of content related to any given search query.

BuzzSumo can perform a variety of content actions, all based on vast sets of data and SERP scraping, but its primary use is providing practical information on content ideas and performance metrics/benchmarking/tracking for social shares, engagement and backlinks.

As generating natural backlinks (on-site content sharing and promotion/placements) are one of the biggest challenges faced by businesses to help new content rank; get discovered; and provide wider topical trust, expertise and authority signals, having data to see what already works is a top trailing indicator to use for reverse engineering new marketing content.

With the paid version, you can look at longer term trends (up to 5 years and as from little as the past 24 hours) for repeat seasonal new content building, plus social performance by platform (Reddit, Twitter, Facebook, more), with the view to break into active topics and discussions.

SEMRush for content ideas, goal setting and competitor research

In fact, SEMRush can be great for all sorts of content brainstorming, comparing your site to competitor websites, identifying content and key term gaps, plus a great deal more.

Practical Tip. If you have not used SEMRush before as part of your content creation and marketing efforts, the main sections I would encourage you to explore are below.

Keyword gap enables you to compare up to five domains, which in most cases will be your site and the top-ranking four external sites on any given topic or product area. Using this SEMRush feature you can select the keyword type you are interested in (I would generally look at Organic Keywords as these are earned and therefore free opportunities), but you can also select paid and others.

You can see common or shared keywords between sites and those unique to you or other domains. My preference is to look initially at shared keywords and then rerun the data with the most unique terms competitor so that I can gather keyword gaps data.

You can also create nice visualisations for easy insights sharing and next actions.

I like to filter out brand terms so that you can look at competitor sites keywords that are ranking based on the close match content, and the more successful content areas and topics their site is appearing for in search. This tells me the main threats coming from my top competing websites as well as the prominent opportunities that are not yet being maximised for my business.

Backlink gap works in the same comparison approach; however, it is telling you the external gaps from your content marketing (link building activities). These data means that you can create on-site content to attract links to cater for current gaps in linkable content as well as building content for placement on external websites too (one of the top three focus areas for Organic Search ranking).

Topic research which, as the name suggests, lets you enter in a key term or topic and then get access to trend information. You can also filter this to countries and regions to tailor the feedback provided to your core audience target areas. The data you receive include subtopics and terms search volume, 'favourite ideas' and trending subtopics, which at the time of writing is still in beta mode.

When you click on a subtopic/key term, you are provided with headlines of top-ranking content and related questions on the topic area, all of which are perfect for refining your potential new content posts and getting started with filling untapped content gaps and opportunity.

Ahrefs for content and keyword exploration, tracking, plus authority impact

The two main paid content creation and exploration tools (within the 20–30 semi-frequently used tools, and the broader 100 plus ad hoc tools) that I use as part of my working life are Ahrefs and SEMRush.

Ahrefs has a content explorer section which works in a similar fashion to SEMRush but uses social media, referring domains, traffic volumes and other factors like domain rating as filter options. I have to say I prefer this to the SEMRush topic data, as I find it more meaningful when it comes down to practical use and direct relevancy for content creation and marketing. Using Ahrefs content explorer, I can see what works and what's trending for topic and apply that logic to the new content that gets created.

If my goal is awareness and social sharing, I will place increased focus on content, attracting the most social shares and backlinks. If the goal is traffic, I can sort by traffic received and often older, more established content and marketing topics.

Choosing the Data Tools You Need

To assist you with future data source selection, you can use the Data Collection Decision Tree provided in this guide. This will help verify that the choices you are

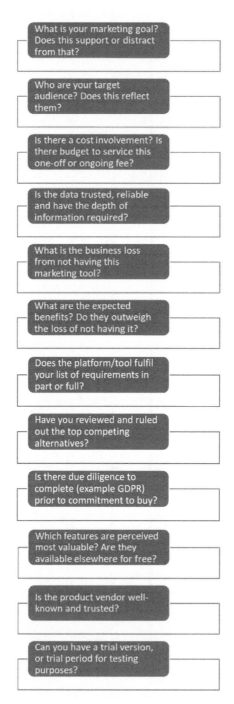

Fig. 3.1.   Data Collection Decision Tree.

making for new tool purchase or use, fulfil the key business needs, plus this can support more objectivity and consistency within your decision process.

Unlike traditional decision tree processes, this example sets out clear aspects of the decision-making process and maps out the stages within your consideration hierarchy to consider each factor.

This will help with ensuring you are giving new data points and sources and more objective and consistent review before making a final judgement on whether to include or exclude them as part of your businesses' big data processes.

If the answer to any of the stages is 'no', you will want to pause any commitment to purchase until that resolves back to a 'yes', or find an alternative data platform that enables you to satisfy every step of the data tool decision tree.

Managing Your Data

Managing your data and factoring in regular data management reviews and integrity checks are an important part of any data-led framework, and data for producing marketing content are no different.

Data management fundamentally falls into the realm of administration and is often a divided task between end users and the development/IT team.

Creating a culture of proactive data management is more difficult than it may first appear, and this is predominantly attached to the monotonous nature of the tasks, added to the fact that outcome is rarely tangible. The people primarily accountable for data management and integrity ('primarily' as every user should have a hand on ability to positively impact this) need to understand the importance of the task at hand and repeatedly allocate time towards maintaining the data.

Everything relies on data integrity. You will likely have heard the phrase 'garbage in garbage out' (GIGO), and this phrase has more direct meaning when associated to data than any other application.

The process for managing your data can include many important stages, but there are a few essential phases which should not be overlooked, and these are mentioned in Fig. 3.2.

When it comes to data management, the process is a cyclical one, repeating continuously, and available for ad hoc actions at any stage of the process, either in isolation and single step or collectively and aggregate/complete level review.

The Data Management Process

There are five distinct threads to the data management process, and these are as follows.

(1) **Identification and gathering** – A discovery phase for understanding what data points the business needs and putting in place measures to gathering said data.
(2) **Classification, definition and normalisation** – Getting the data ready for use and through a processing phase. This is about the application of automated rules and business logic.

(3) **Accessibility, application and quality** – How fit the data are for their intended purpose. Issues identified at this stage require redressing prior to moving forward.

(4) **Worth, operability and usefulness** – At this stage, incorporating a degree of beta testing with end users can be a useful exercise. You can be asking the following questions: are the data meaningful? Can the end user easily complete actions from the data? Are there data gaps or use problems (for example, exporting the data, filtering it and deriving intended use)?

(5) **Governance, refinement and improvements** – Matching current data outcomes with required business needs, proactive measurement and monitoring of other data steps, plus continuous improvement methodology supporting ongoing gains.

Common Data Actions

There are many varied actions that get undertaken by staff accountable for data management.

Some of the more typical tasks assigned to data management stakeholders include the following:

- Benchmarking, analysis and improvement to technology infrastructure
- Policing, maintenance and implementation of data policies and procedures
- Ongoing data collection, identification and efficient processing
- Implementation of automated data processes
- Key staff steering meetings and feedback protocols for continuous improvements

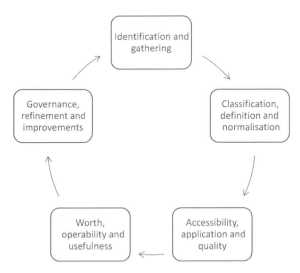

Fig. 3.2. Data Management Process Diagram.

- Building of intelligent algorithms and other easy data insights applications
- Functionality checks, updates and data improvements/exclusions
- Feedback frameworks for proactive 'all-user' knowledge sharing and improvement ideation
- Security, confidentiality, integrity work
- Value, purpose and broader requirement fulfilment
- Team training, insights sharing and efficiency including documented use and tooltips

The Role of GDPR

The European Union (EU) General Data Protection Regulation (GDPR) update that was seen enforceable in 2018 is the most important change when it comes to data privacy regulation over the past two decades for any company operating within the EU.

It took four years of extended discussion and refinement prior to GDPR being approved by the EU Parliament back in April 2016.

The GDPR 2016/679 places new regulation on EU law for data protection and privacy. This added regulation is in place for all individuals within the EU as well as the European Economic Area (EEA).

GDPR has an added role of addressing the exporting of personal data outside the EU and EEA.

Before you read on, it's important that I categorically state that I am not a legal expert or GDPR specialist. Any and all of the points raised in this section of this marketing content guide are solely based on my personal interpretation of research papers, guides and other publicly accessible information pertinent to my individual GDPR understanding.

You should always seek expert and relevant legal representation when it comes to highly specialist subject matters including GDPR. The information that follows is not intended as direct, actionable guidance, it is simply to support the understanding of GDPR as a broader topic of note which you should be aware of when considering the application and gathering of data (plus other matters) for you and your business.

The information that follows should be seen as an overview of how I have understood the role of GDPR at the time of writing this segment of the book, and not in any means, an attempt to provide direct instructions on how you should interpret GDPR in relation to your unique business and your data situation.

An Overview of GDPR

GDPR replaced the previous Data Protection Directive 95/46/EC with objectives including solidifying data privacy laws across Europe, protecting and empowering data privacy for people within the EU and reshaping the way companies spanning the EU and EEA approach the privacy of people's data.

A large part of GDPR pertains to the consent from the individual about the collection, processing and use of their data, and whilst GDPR builds on many of the pre-existing data privacy directives in place, there are new factors to be aware of. It is worth completing supplemental research into GDPR (if you haven't already done so) as well as seeking professional, legal advice on the subject matter, so that you can ensure your business is meeting the requirements as they currently stand.

There is a useful European Commission GDPR resource available online at the time of writing at https://ec.europa.eu/commission/priorities/justice-and-fundamental-rights/data-protection/2018-reform-eu-data-protection-rules_en, which will assist your understanding of GDPR.

The intended benefits of GDPR is that for individuals, people get to have increased control over their personal data, and for businesses, companies in the EU/EEA all have the same, consistent set of rules to follow.

As a business, there are numerous parts to GDPR that you will need to take note of. These include (not exhaustively) those detailed below.

This will give you a solid overview of some of the many factors that come into effect with GDPR:

- Better communication with people. Clearly stating who you are, why you are processing their data, how long you intend to keep the data for, and confirming who will get the data
- Obtaining consent for processing people's data. Important fields within this are having a legitimate business interest, legal obligations and clear consent
- Enabling people to access to data stored/processed/collected
- Providing with updates on any data risks or breaches
- 'Right to be forgotten' including the deletion and removal of personal data upon request
- Profiling within applications that are legally binding need customers to be informed, human process checking for refusals, plus the right for people to contest failed applications
- Including opt out rights for everyone when it comes to direct marketing use
- Protecting and safeguarding personal data and information including health, race, sexual orientation and more
- Obtaining parental consent for minors and anyone under the age of 16 years (this can also change related to the country/member state within the EU)
- Legal arrangements for data transfers to countries outside of the EU (not approved by the EU authorities)

Each of the above consideration areas will apply to your business regardless of how you are collecting data and creating or sending marketing content.

Chapter Summary

This chapter explored the practicalities of gathering and managing data and divulged many great free (plus some useful paid for) platforms and software packages for generating increased business data and associated insights for building your competitive data-driven marketing content edge.

In this section, we introduced many practical tips of using suggested tools and data sources so that you can hit the ground running regardless of experience or expertise level working with data, or using specific tools.

Some unique and new visual aids were developed for this guide to help you to choose the best marketing content tools for your business, plus a framework that will assist with managing your increased data.

The third dominant subject matter covered in this section of the guide was the role of GDPR in creating marketing content. In 2018, GDPR has been one of the foremost challenges for businesses of all sizes related to data collection and use, so this was an important informational field of note.

It is important that if you have not already done so, your business seeks specialist legal/professional advice for GDPR advice and support. This chapter simply discussed some of the main informational elements of GDPR that are publicly accessible at the time of writing and cannot be construed as any form of advice.

As we progress into the next chapter, this practical guide moves onto the topic of transforming data into marketing content, such as the matters of understanding your audience, deriving data insights and creating your content action plans.

Definitions

- Data management: the process of reviewing, storing, maintaining and organising your data so that they are able to match the needs of your business.
- Data integrity: the accuracy, validity and consistency of data being referenced. Without data integrity, none of the actins and insights derived from data can be relied upon.
- Data refinement: this includes the removal on unrequired and incorrect data, the normalisation of disparate data sets so that recombined meanings can be gathered, plus redundancy and variability focus.
- GDPR: the General Data Protection Regulation is the primary European law which regulates personal data protection.
- Personal data: any information that enables you to identify a specific person or related to an identified individual. This could be as simply as collecting name and address information or broader social information.

Chapter 4

Transforming Data into Content

It is the data transformation process that carves and cultivates your company's competitive content advantage, moving you away from reactive and restrictive content building, and towards prescriptive and proactive marketing content that fuels success.

Having easy access to trustworthy deeper data sets permits your business to begin this process, and throughout this section of the guide, we walk you through the practical approaches for creating content reflective of your audience, gleaning insights from information, and creating content action plans and support repeatable results.

Understanding Your Audience

Every piece of content created must have an intended audience. Whether that audience is a single influencers buy-in or 1 million new users landing on a website a month, you will always fail to deliver optimum results if you are not audience aware.

Audience inertia with writing content that reflects the user's wants and needs is more common with small- to medium-sized businesses than any other.

Central questions listed below need to be at the forefront of your strategic content mindset before putting pen to paper:

- Who are we talking to, and what are we looking to achieve through talking to them (does this differ to who we want to be talking to)?
- What content do our current and potential customers digest? How do can we act on this?
- What audience pain points can we solve? What stages in the user journey is this most evident?
- What motivates our target audience? How can we impact their motivations more effectively?
- What are our audience sharing, engaging with and talking about? Has that changed over time? Are new trends occurring?
- Where to do target users go for their industry news, insights and information? Are you present in those forums, aggregator websites, and wider social conversations?

Data-driven Marketing Content, 51–65
Copyright © 2019 by Emerald Publishing Limited
All rights of reproduction in any form reserved
doi:10.1108/978-1-78973-817-920191005

The overriding understanding with your audience should be the following: How much do we and can we know about our audience? and How can we turn this insight into effective content writing and delivery?

Understanding Your Audience Through Data

In this part of the guide, we look practically at several specific processes that you can follow to gather increased audience understanding through freely available data sources discussed within earlier chapters of this book.

There are many ways in which any organisation can look to shape fresh audience insights (customer surveys, forms, focus groups, social media competitions, competitor analysis, face-to-face meetings, front line telesales staff feedback, etc.), but for the purposes of this part of the book, the focus sits solely with deriving audience insights from free data packages (analytics platforms).

A common outcome from revisiting audience observations and formulating deeper audience awareness are audience personas – something we also provide towards the end of this chapter.

Google Analytics Audience Overview Reports

The audience reports section of your Google Analytics (GA) account can be accessed directly from the persistent navigation on the left-hand side, intuitively named 'Audience'.

From here you can drill down into audience overview level information which you can split by the main metrics groups (traffic, new users, users, bounce rates, more), compare year on year with previous period, and get a to-level view of how your audience are engaging with your website.

You can grasp the divide between new and returning people, the amount of content they consume on your site, how long they spend on a session and how many of them exit the site (or bounce) without competing a single action, or extra page view.

At overview stages, you can also get single click access to audience demographics, systems used, plus mobile data.

Beta stage (so far from ideal as yet, though worth noting all the same) include lifetime value of a user, that provides value per user and lifetime revenue stats which can help justify marketing spend and digital investment.

There is also cohort analysis reporting user explorer, as well as audiences.

Practical Tip. Get familiar with 'User Explorer' as this enables you to examine individual user behaviour at visit (session) level.

These data are perfect for isolating, targeting and growing your perfect user! As an example of this in action:

- Login to your GA account
- Go to Audience > User Explorer
- Pick out the ideal user (for example, the user who has a low bounce rate and a high number of transactions and revenue)
- Click on the Client Id provided inside GA

When you see the normalised data, you can take action on it.

Review the pages viewed in each session, the time of day they entered the site, and other behavioural items including device used to enter the site, channel/ medium they came from, plus any other contributing data points which you can use for content creation, placement and channel promotion.

From knowing the above, you can do the following:

- Ensure that each common page viewed in the ideal customer journey is optimised and driving them to the sale
- Reduce exits on those pages and encourage click through rate (CTR)
- Minimise the average number of pages viewed and clicks made between landing page and conversion page (merging related pages where possible)
- Optimise the user flow and performance of related pages (speed, functionality, mobile friendliness, other)
- Begin to piece together the informational, educational and transactional requirements and barriers to be overcome to attract and convert more of the perfect buyer

This summary stage insight is of value but is barely the tip of the information iceberg.

GA Audience Demographics, Interests and Locations

Once you enable demographics and interests in your GA account, you can view, analyse and start to build your audience personas as well as compare and contrast them to your ideal audience personas.

You can view gender splits, highest impact age groups, affinity categories, hobbies, more, then visualise how this has changed over time (comparing with previous period or previous years), plus filter all of this by key measurements (metric areas).

Anyone involved in marketing will also be eager to use the location data (which has country, city, region and subcontinent information). For content building, pitching and refining, the location data are ideal.

This means that you can prioritise cities/countries and tailor content (plus create new pages/information) to become richer destination landing pages, reflecting the audience language nuances, regional dialect and other factors that reinforce location-based user expectations.

Increased Audience Awareness Through Google Analytics

Other data insights worth exploration at this time through GA include behaviour, technology, cross-device and benchmarking reports. These are all accessible from the same audience section.

Do not limit yourself to the aforementioned audience segmentation reports in GA, but certainly pay added attention to them.

When logged into your GA account, navigate to Audience > Behaviour. A couple of the most frequent segments I use practically with building new business content include the following:

- 'New vs Returning – New users will need much more guidance and support to convert, while repeat users will want to expedite the journey as much as possible.
- Conversion Probability – To drill down into the likelihood of a user converting within a 30-day period. The transactions for all users are evaluated and a probability of conversion score is provided – expressed as an average score of 1–100 (100 being the highest).

One of the exciting and more advanced techniques to use with GA is working with segments. When you start using GA data segmentation, you can recombine data sets and generate additional insights.

Working with the previous example of conversion probability, you can see which channels have the highest likelihood of conversion and can demand greater budget allocation. You can also determine how many new or repeat users you need to land on your website to hit new sales targets (and what age groups you should prioritise first).

Building Audience Personas

An important output of any comprehensive audience analysis is the audience persona.

Put simply, personas are accurate representations of your customers. While they tend to represent ideal customers you are targeting, they can also reflect current or historical types of people relevant to the business.

Common persona segmentation options are covered now.

- Overview/summary – An easy to share and understandable description on the person
- Goals and motivations – What drives your audience to act?
- Interests and hobbies – The things that excite them and the topics they gravitate to
- Marketing channels – The sources and mediums they interact with the most
- Brands and affinities – Which companies and products reflect them
- Professional bio – The business group, professional qualities and business affiliations they have

An important aspect of audience personas is building a real-world picture of the individuals you are focussing on as the primary business generators (existing and/or aspirational).

Within a few moments, anyone in your business should be able to understand what your customers look like (their main characteristics) and how to impact them in a positive way.

The predominant goal of audience personas is effective pitching, targeting, marketing, and promotion of content to ensure it represents the wants and needs of primary target audiences throughout the information seeking and buying funnels.

Effective audience personas mean that all the important stakeholders in your organisation are working towards the same identified people content outcomes. This supports increased effectivity, consistency of messaging and integration plus alignment of frequently disperse marketing departments and specialist business units.

Anyone new to a business, irrespective of experience or role, should be able to quickly identify and understand who matters the most to your business when it comes to sales and revenue groups.

Many elements of data-driven content for marketing purpose can feel removed from the audience as you are using metrics, stats and other normalised data; however, audience personas put the people to the foreground – something which should never be omitted.

Here you can see audience profiling through the use of personas in action.

Overview	Goals/ Motivations	Interests	Marketing Channels	Brands
Mid-30s, married, male who is a senior level marketing professional, living in the UK and has a young family. Age: 35 Marital status: Married Job: Senior Marketing Manager Location: London, UK	• Eating healthier and exercising more • Setting and achieving yearly challenges • Experiencing new things with my family and friends • Career progression	Interests: sports, family, lifestyle, technology Affinity categories: food, travel, technology, media	• Organic Search/SEO • Social Media Marketing: • LinkedIn • Twitter • Facebook • Industry forums • PR/UK Media • Content Marketing	Sport: Nike, Adidas, Under Armour Clothing: Ted Baker, Paul Smith, Levis Lifestyle: Google, Disney, Netflix, BBC News, Land Rover, Amazon, Jaguar
Early retiree, married, female, living in the UK,	• Spending quality time with family and friends	Interests: Family, lifestyle, community	• Direct marketing • Resellers	Community: Local media Clothing: M&S,

(Continued)

Overview	Goals/ Motivations	Interests	Marketing Channels	Brands
with an adult family. Age: 55 Marital status: Married Job: Retire volunteer Location: West Sussex, UK	• Looking after grand-children, pro-gressing their development • Supporting the local community with volun-teering time and experience	Affinity categories: food, travel, home and garden	• PR/UK Media • Referral	Peacocks, Bonmarche Lifestyle: Holland & Barrett, Specsavers, Hallmark, Jessops, B&Q

Here's an example of what a finished persona may look like:

Lee Wilson (Bio)	Interests, Goals and Motivations	Channels and Brands
Mid-thirties, married, male who is a senior level marketing professional, living in the UK, and has a young family. Age: 35 Marital status: Married Job: Senior Marketing Manager Location: London, UK  'I like all things digital, dividing my time between sports, family, writing, and work.'	**Goals:** • Eating healthier and exercising more • Setting and achieving yearly challenges • Experiencing new things with my fam-ily and friends • Career progression **Interests:** Interests: Sports, family, lifestyle Affinity categories: Food, travel, technol-ogy, media 'I'm self-motivated and care about personal, family and professional achievements. I want to challenge myself and enjoy life, and explore.'	**Marketing Channels:** • Organic Search/SEO • Social Media Marketing: • LinkedIn • Twitter • Facebook • Industry forums • PR/UK Media • Content Marketing **Brands:** Sport: Nike, Adidas, Under Armour Clothing: Ted Baker, Paul Smith, Levis Lifestyle: Google, Dis-ney, Netflix, BBC News, Land Rover, Amazon, Jaguar 'I believe in quality, seeking out information and brands I trust.'

Deriving Data Insight

The end goal of transforming data into result-orientated marketing content can only be realised through effective mechanisms and approaches towards gathering repeatable and actionable data-based insights.

Data forms the trusted, realisable and ongoing (fresh) input, whilst actionable insights deliver the creative, new, exciting and tangible next steps to enhance your marketing content and refine the results achieved – Without one you cannot have the other.

There are many companies stuck between the stages of gathering lots of data and access to numerous analytical packages, but still failing to get to the stage where they are gathering meaningful data insights.

To define 'insights', this refers to the value obtained through the use of deep (big) data. To clarify this further, the type of value (or insights) gained are intended to have practical application, and therefore we are looking at actionable insights from data.

When you combine data-driven, actionable insights with marketing content creation, you are able to accomplish amazing business results.

To set expectations, every insight will not be a huge light-bulb moment, and in fact they shouldn't be. If you are only looking for the 'wow' moment, you are ignoring the hundreds of tweaks, updates and refinements that will cumulatively make a massive difference to your business and marketing efforts.

An actionable insight may be something as simple as finding a new demand in buyer trending search behaviour or identifying a new product variation to add to a range based on your websites onsite search use, and queries that do not have a current product that are being searched for.

If we break down data, analytics and insights, we can see the following:

Data/information – The metric and measurement detail collected. For example – your home page received 3,000 visits yesterday.

Analytics – Building on the data layer, analytics provides added context, trends and data points to analyse and inform. For example – Your home page received 3,000 visits yesterday, compared with last year this is a 20% reduction, plus new users on this page are bouncing more (15% extra bounces on the same timeframe).

Insights – The effective use of data and analytics to make positive changes based on the application of the analytics and data available. For example – after completing further analysis of the types of visitors landing on the home page, we can tell that the business has lost half of the 25- to 34-year-old age group after removing video content from the home page. By reincorporating this, we would expect to increase engagement (reducing bounce rates) and reattract the younger audience (through effective video promotion and page quality signals).

The next level of data-led insights are 'prescriptive insights' – detailed now.

Prescriptive insights – The proactive data-driven provision of new insights to identified staff/specialists, for drip feeding of new potential actions based on new data additions and existing data set changes/updates. This practically means that, every time new data are available (every hours and day, in the case of GA, GSC and other data sources mentioned earlier in this guide), intelligent algorithms will be advising you of opportunities (and potentially threats) to take action on. The fundamental change from 'insights' to 'prescriptive insights' is that insights rely primarily on the user to look for something, whereas prescriptive insights volunteer actions to the user regardless of human involvement or availability and intent to act.

This is not where data-driven insights end though – the next section practically explores a number of main insight types you can be factoring into your data-driven marketing content approaches.

Types of Data-led Insight

When it comes to data-driven insights that are directly applicable to improving business marketing content, there are thousands of distilled examples that can be provided.

The following are some of the insights you may wish to explore; however, please do not limit yourself to these alone, as the opportunity is substantially greater.

- **Measurement insights.** You may have lots of data, but without examining the potential data gaps, and defining the core metrics that matter most to your business, you will always limit the impact of the insights derived. Things to consider include leading and trailing measurements, highest impact channels, hypothesis that you cannot currently answer with your data, highest impact metrics (impressions, traffic, CTR, events, goal completions, phone calls, revenue, average order values, term and topic exposure and business share).
- **Contextual insights.** Statistics and data without context, or understood user placement of the data within the remits of the intended business purpose and priority outcomes, undermine the insights delivered. If you have clearly separate end user groups, with different and unique end goals and applications from the data, they should be seeing very different data views, not expected to glean the same level of insights form a single access view of all the data. Ability to export data is useful for additional analytics, but for insights purposes, all data requires contextualisation and positioning reflective of purpose and desired outcome.
- **Specificity insights.** The more that the insights are specific, detailed and defined, the increased likelihood of them being acted on and implemented. Often a combined outcome of measurement and contextual insight approaches, specificity insight projects comprehensively explain the wider information needed to effectively deliver the insights.
- **Novelty and curiosity insights.** Overlooked often based on the increased perceived importance of known insight-driven projects, novelty and curiosity

insights-based campaigns are designed to be more interesting and compelling. These can sometimes provide the eureka moments and stem creative next actions outside of the traditional action plans.

- **Stakeholder and alignment insights.** Ask questions, request form/survey answers, run group sessions. You need to understand, distil, evaluate, expand and often challenge, what the key staff barriers, expectations, pain points, and aspiration are. Marketing content insights can impact internal sentiment, budget allocation and other direct factors, limiting or supporting your ability to perform.

- **Audience insights.** We have discussed GA audience segmentation in some detail earlier in this chapter. Segmentation is about seeing, understanding, and impacting key audience groups through increased data insights. The more you know about current, potential, and changing audiences that matter most to your business, the more you can create impactful business content and marketing messaging. If your business is failing to convert specific age groups, you need to fix that situation. If the top five product pages on your website are converting fewer visitors into customers, you need to be able to change that.

- **Visualisation insights.** Data visualisation will massively impact the amount of people who can proactively contribute towards data insights as well as the volume of ongoing actions attributed to data insights. There are many barriers in place when you take the journey from data towards insights, and data visualisation is one of the most important ones. Analytics packages can help overcome this, as can extensions to them (consider Google Studio). Microsoft PowerBi is well worth review as a paid option for pulling in lots of segmented data sets into one place and creating interactive data visualisations (easy to understand and act on tables, charts, graphs and visuals), Google Studio another free version.

- **Refinement insights.** The data-driven opportunity is never static. Everyone interacting with your data needs to have the ability to positively influence it. Refinement insights are based on effective review, measure, and refine controls, combined with simple feedback mechanisms in place to collect, prioritise, and implement updates. Key staff user group meetings help regularly can act as the small focus group decision makers to control the 'decision by committee' dilemma which can occur with unchecked easy feedback facilitation.

- **Descriptive insights.** Where diagnostic insight is about the 'why', descriptive is focused on the 'what'. The specifics tied to what happened, what changed, and more importantly what to do about it. The data are historical information with the outcome being insights to impact future performance.

- **Prescriptive insights.** As described previously in this chapter, the focus is on proactive and actionable insights identification and sharing based on pre-defined parameters. This changes with every new data source and data set. Prescriptive insights suggest actions based on known data, following given processes to a specific outcome.

- **Diagnostic insights.** Focussed on understanding what's happened based on a change or questions you might already have. Here you are looking for insights of why something happened. This may be performance declines on pages, rankings, sales and other metrics, or looking at dependencies of one change, channel or update made on other factors and business areas.
- **Predictive insights.** Looking forward and asking yourself what could happen. This can combine the findings of both descriptive and diagnostic insights (what happened and why it happened) to forecast forward what might or could happen. The important thing to remember at this stage is the action characteristic of insight. Knowing what might happen can empower you to taken action and impact the insight. For example, by using historical product sales data, I can use all existing data to predict seasonal trends and product demand. By knowing this I can increase stock, add and promote website marketing content, create product discounts that reflect current interest, and more.

Practical Tip. There are many ways to act on and implement big data insights and some of my favourite quick tips and actions used are below, which can help you consider the comprehensive picture and even replicate some of these today.

- Have a clearly defined goal of what you want to achieve. This will help refine the scope of the project and how the data relate to the wider business goals. The more specific, this is the better. Your challenge is often not getting the data to gain insight from, it is refining what you actively include and focus on to impact the business.
- By focussing more on the outcome people tend to deliver the outputs faster. This is regularly reflective of the enthusiasm of the team about what they are going to achieve. When reverse engineering the win, you can also organise and add to data sets that are end goal oriented.
- Data quality is paramount. This guide mentioned previously about 'garbage in garbage out' (GIGO), and it cannot be overstated that as your data grow, and you rely on it more, the integrity, quality and ongoing maintenance of it, have to be at the fore.
- Integrating different specialists and specialisms for project-based campaigns will improve the outcome. Businesses can gain marketing content multiplier effects by removing integrated skills working together and expanding the wider business contribution towards marketing content outputs.
- Customer centricity matters more than most things. Behind every item of business content created, there is a person (almost always a potential customer) reading, viewing and digesting it. If there is a single perspective that matters more than any other, it is the customers. Your data tell you everything you need to know about customer content engagement,

stratification, motivation, plus so much more; however, you need to use and prioritise it.

- As you start growing your business importance of big data and expanding the company approach and culture to incorporate increased data-driven emphasis, you should consider the internal and/or external talent required to facilitate getting the most from this change. Expert role including data analysts and data scientists are becoming increasingly popular (and important) to businesses. If budget is not available for in-house talent acquisition at this time, you may wish to look at search, digital and marketing agency support to fill this need.

Creating Content Action Plans

A content action plan sets out and clearly defines the specific actions required to deliver on an end goal or objective area.

Regardless of the objective, the action plan provides the timeline of activities required to get to the desired outcome.

An effective action plan (or timelined roadmap) benefits the delivery of projects on time via a more thorough assessment of the milestones and individual stages needed to complete the campaign (and body of work).

Tools for Content Action Plans

There are a myriad of free and paid tools, plus software applications suitable for formulating, delivering and refining a marketing content action plan.

Personally, I prefer to keep it simple.

My requirements for an action plan include the following:

- Easy to log actions
- Version control tracking
- Varied permission setting (view, edit, etc.)
- Collaboration support
- Simple and effective templating

Preferences for business content action plan creation include Google sheets (Excel, for simple updates and collaboration), Trello (for action setting and completion plus tracking through the process), ToodleDo (for reminders and chasing up deadlines), plus standard Microsoft packages and Teams for ongoing communications over distance, as well as refining actions, sending feedback and policing agreed outputs.

Features of Marketing Content Action Plans

There are consistent characteristics that every action plan should include to support more effective and efficient delivery to goal business content projects. These are discussed next and provided as a content action plan template.

Project lead (PL). Every project must assign an individual accountable for the final (complete) delivery of the work. The project lead can be seen as the account manager within typical agency environments, assuming the accountability for the totality of the project, even thought most of the action completion will be fulfilled by the wider team. Common PL duties include the following:

- Defining the project objective
- Setting and clarifying project goals and objectives
- Providing meaningful (SMART) success benchmarks and expected outcomes
- Setting up and running project meetings
- Assigning actions, deadlines and accountability to staff
- Documenting project progression and action status
- Reporting and presenting progress
- Reviewing and refining approach

Project goals. SMART goals: specific, measurable, agreed upon, realistic and time-based.

Action. The task plus detail with a level of information supplied for direct action taking.

Expected time. The amount of time assigned to the task. This sets expectations and time demands.

Start date/end date. Expectations (pre-agreed, as opposed to dictated) on when to commence and deliver assigned actions.

Task owner. The individuals assigned and accountable for completing the actions and activities agreed upon at project start and updated in planned project review stages.

Task status. Usually predefined in the action plan document as not started, in progress, complete.

Priority. Confirming the importance of the action to the project success. Normally this is high, medium and low, but it can be more granular and numeric.

Associated metrics, benchmarks and desired outcomes. Detailing 'what good looks like', 'where we are' and 'how we measure it'.

Comments. Free format notes pertinent to the action, left by the task owner primarily.

Progression overview. Visualisation (usually percentage driven chart) clarifying the expected and actual progress relating the current situation back to the expected project timeline. This often sits as a supplemental coversheet.

Example Marketing Content Action Plan

Here's an example of the complete action plan for simple replication. A blank template is also provided for direct use.

Project Lead (PL): Lee Wilson	Project Goal: By 21 November 2020, implement a new community content resource. This will include five topic sections. This is expected to provide 15,000 Organic monthly impressions in Google UK, 1,000 monthly visits and 500 new users to the website per month from Organic, Direct and Referral channels combined.							
Action	**Time**	**Owner**	**Priority**	**Status**	**Start Date**	**Deadline**	**Metrics**	**Comments**
Create version 1 topic landing page framework	1 day	Rob T.	High	In progress	01 July 2020	21 July 2020	N/a	Refer to content brief for details.
Create content for the first topic landing page (location page)	0.5 days	Sarah J.	High	Not started	22 July 2020	30 July 2020	Minimum word count 2,000	As per landing page framework and agreed subtopic coverage areas.
Provide visuals for each segment of the agreed first landing page (location page)	0.5 days	Andy G.	Medium	Not started	22 July 2020	30 July 2020	Six images needed; one banner, five segment images	As per audience persona, tone, style and pitch report provided.

Blank action plan:

Project Lead (PL):	Project Goal:							
Action	Time	Owner	Priority	Status	Start Date	Deadline	Metrics	Comments

Chapter Summary

The dominant theme of this chapter explored practical means for progressing your marketing content efforts from the data stage through to insights derived.

Practical provisions included the following:

- Audience understanding step by steps
- Audience persona template and example
- Content action plan template

Moving onto the next chapter, you will discover why your content is failing to deliver results, how to overcome common content pain points and the practicalities of bridging and integrating distinct mediums for multiplying returns.

Definitions

- Persona: a fictional characterisation of key people groups most important to your business. Many companies create several audience persona models driven by business data and research into the highest perceived value audience segments.

- Marketing channels: these are the people, companies and actions involved to move a service, product or ownership area from production to consumption. Marketing channels include SEO, PPC, Twitter, Offline advertising and more.
- Audience demographics: this is the segmentation, classification and grouping of identified people groups through shared characteristics.

Chapter 5

Understanding Why Your Content Isn't Working

Marketing content has the fundamental purpose of engaging and interacting with your target audience.

Regardless of all the other metric-based goals and objectives you have from the business content being created, if you are not achieving the right type of interactions with your key audience personas, your content is failing.

There are 2,190 million Google UK search results for the query 'why content doesn't work', so realistically, if you are confident that your content is working, then you are the exception and not the rule.

Overcoming Content Pain Points

There are 10 main reasons why marketing and wider content disappoints to deliver on results, and we investigate these in more detail now.

Why Does Content Fail?

It would be easy to avoid this question, reflect on the myriad of potential skewing factors and summarise failure to unique company oversights and inadequacies, but in most situations, this simply isn't the case.

(1) **Insufficient planning.** Lack of planning and inadequate allowance for preparation within content building restrict success. Content frequently is seen as a quick fix and reactive marketing approach. This is fundamentally flawed and needs to change. The top performing content is planned substantially ahead of time. It is no coincidence that some of the most authoritative and valuable content has been ranking in search engines for a number of years, covers subject matters comprehensively and gets refreshed and revisited every year. When you commit to creating best of breed business and marketing content, you need to increase delivery times and account for a substantially more thorough planning and preparation phase of work. Poor planning is quoted as the project management number one mistake – this holds true for failed content too.

Data-driven Marketing Content, 67–79
Copyright © 2019 by Emerald Publishing Limited
All rights of reproduction in any form reserved
doi:10.1108/978-1-78973-817-920191006

(2) **Strategic shortfalls.** Aligned with planning, strategy can all too often make or break a content campaign. In the previous chapter, we discussed the factors for effective content plans and the requirement for setting and sharing project goals. Content writers need to be strategically guided, ensuring that the end goal is always in mind throughout the content building process.

(3) **Absent storytelling.** Business has prioritised volume content building over purposeful content creation. The numbers game in marketing content has meant that there is massively increased content noise in every market and very little being said. The content that 'naturally' performs has clear messaging, a reason for being, plus a story to tell. It is no coincidence that the John Lewis Christmas television campaigns trend every year before anybody even knows what the content is! Stories sell.

(4) **Internal emphasis.** If you are designing content with a singular focus on your internal environment only, excluding all of the external factors (completing content, external data, industry trends, more), you will often miss the actual opportunity and be implementing content for you rather than your audience. You may try to dismiss this as an automatic requirement your business satisfies, but I urge you to look at the last 10 business content items your company has built and ask yourself 'who is this piece written for?' I guarantee in many situations you will discover people writing for and to themselves. This is ironic (notably for marketing content) and a repeated business failure.

(5) **Ineffective conversion mechanisms.** In some cases, generating end results from content has very little to do with the content itself. Content can drive many people to a landing page, yet the same people interested to click/ engage/act in the first place fail to proceed to any event-based goal completion. Assuming that the content purpose, pitch and targeting was supportive of generating new business leads or other macro goal completions (unlikely to be a typical blog post or news story, as an example), and people fail to convert, the issue lies outside of the content and within the process you are driving them. Inability to identify and improve inadequacies throughout the conversion process will massively reduce your content marketing outcomes.

(6) **Overlooking SEO.** Search Engine Optimisation (SEO) can account for upwards of 40% of all traffic, sales and other business metrics for most, if not all, businesses. The primary reason why SEO has such a mammoth potential content impact is because it focuses on the data as a descriptive content feeder. SEO experts rely on search behaviour, competitive analysis, search trends, keyword volumes, reverse engineering top competing content, plus an entire suite of extra data-fuelled measurements to create harder working content. SEO is not an isolated content success factor, but it must form part of the content ideation, building, refinement and measurement team. An SEO expert worth their salt, makes all things better, stronger, faster – content being at the foreground. If you consider content as king, then the role of SEO is one of the royal advisor.

(7) **Budget.** Content that has paid marketing budget behind it (paid content promotion, paid social media, paid content remarketing, etc.) will always return increased impact and results than marketing content without paid budget allocation. Bigger paid marketing budgets will return larger returns. The return on advertising spend (ROAS) will not always be proportional, especially when trying to push result volumes within higher spend areas, but budget always plays a critical part in success. You can increase creativity, novelty, insight, conversion rate optimisation (CRO), and a myriad more, but doing the same with increased budget will derive increased gains. Extra budget directly drives increased exposure. Where possible, try to be objective with budget allocation and incorporate external competitor spend within the process for concluding your own spend levels. Large budget disparities cause would be content wins to fall short.

(8) **Mispositioning.** Content positioning and placement quickly become neglected once business content writing becomes overly process driven and formulaic. Indicators that this is happening include placing the product/service and marketing messaging before the purpose and problem the products/services solve. You will see this commented on as being 'lazy marketing' as normally this is deemed as quicker content creation, but in many cases, it is a habitual rather than neglect based. New users seeing your content for the first time are driven by self-interest and personal problem-solving first. It is only later in the consideration phase of action that product/service/brand and supplemental comparative factors come into play.

(9) **Content promotion.** The correct headline, subject matter, research, data, content pitch and other content characteristics only serve a partial value if the appropriate time and expert resource is not applied to promoting the content. Even the biggest brands need to spend an equal amount of time promoting their content as they do creating it. From paid to owned and earned media, there are hundreds of content marketing promotion approaches that can push your business content in front of the correct people.

(10) **Quality.** All content is not equal. A blog post can be a thin value, 50 word, poorly conceptualised, time restricted piece of content, scraped from another website. A blog post can also be an audience inclusive, data-drive, deep content, thought leadership, problem-solving cornerstone topic for your website. Rarely does low-quality content deliver disproportionate results. Frequency, volume and speed of marketing content delivery almost never overrule quality. A well-researched evergreen content article, which provides new insights, opinion and depth of topical coverage (consider expertise, authority and trust (EAT) content defined previously in this guide) can be considered the baseline for all business critical content subject matters.

Future Proofing Your Content

Taking a strategic step back from the 10 content failure fundamentals discussed previously, it is possible to put in place mechanisms which support more robust and disappointment resistant content.

Complacency in business content writing is almost always a precursor to reduced content results. The notion that what worked in the last quarter, or previous seasonal period, will work again for the next one, is languid marketing, and needs redressing. Content writing inertia is easy to fall into but a real-world challenge to avoid. If you have in-house marketing and content writing expertise, it is likely that content creation complacency will impact you more often and to a greater extent.

In no small part, this is related to the fact that in-house marketing content experts start to believe that they inherently know what works, as they expand their understanding of what key staff like the most, what content sails through compliance departments faster, and what content has the least friction through wider company buy-in.

Whilst this growing internal content confidence will expedite content delivery, it will also stagnate progress and dwindle returns from marketing content over time.

By contrast, what an agency losses when it comes to internal process awareness and company understanding, it certainly makes up for when it comes to the continual drive to challenging the status quo and questioning how, what and why marketing content decisions are being made.

The focus of an agency is ultimately to demonstrate progress towards and to deliver upon, business goals and objectives. This can empower agencies to ask the difficult question, experiment more and lead the way with new content approaches and ideas.

The ability for a specialist content agency to draw upon its wider content creation experiences, larger customer base and integrate various expertise areas into one content campaign, also supports it's ability to justify more varied and refined content approaches.

Time restrictions should not be seen as an excuse towards delivering exceptional content, nonetheless expectations need to be realistic too. If your company wants to produce the best example of marketing content on the Internet, within offline magazines, or for a paid marketing campaign, there is a need to support that level of expectation with the applicable amount of time and delivery support, to do so.

There is little more frustrating to content experts than a gulf between delivery scheduling and content expectations.

This type of time limitation can be easily spotted with the content output such as:

- Evidence of editorial process
- Content writer sentiment
- Frequency of spelling and grammatical errors
- Limited content scope and coverage
- Inadequate citing of sources
- Reduced inclusion of statistics and external resources
- A myriad of other received quality restrictions

Technology can be a price, plus expertise and identification barrier for companies, especially those where every penny counts, and each pound invested has heavy scrutiny on what is expected to be returned.

The notion of 'learning' being the investment return over financial gain is a challenging pill to swallow; however, there has to be technological advancement in content creation, the same as in all other business units.

For business of all sizes, investment, trial and experimentation in technology for content building need to be factored into the quarterly company expenditure.

A company failing to embrace new technology is losing out on efficiencies and insights which are restricting its ability to effectively compete and encouraging content lethargy as discussed previously.

Micromanagement suffocates most company specialisms when left unchecked. Content creators by nature need to feel a sense of freedom and creativity in expression to produce their best work. Increasing content specialists autonomy and accountability, not only for the content being the output but also for the content contribution towards the goals and metric-based needs, will provide stringent expected performance levels, without the need to dictate the process to get there.

Topical blindness is effectively a content writer expressing their mental over-exposure to a topic. When content producers are asked and expected to create unique, interesting and engaging content over the long haul, it can quickly become a chore and the notion of topical blindness creeps in. Telltale signs of topical blindness tend to be in throwaway comments like 'there's nothing exciting to write about', 'there's no new information to share' and 'we've covered everything of note'.

None of these statements will ever be factually correct, and in almost every scenario, this will be a writer limitation and creative annoyance, as opposed to any informational barrier that they are faced with.

Industries like the financial services sector where there are tougher restrictions on what can and cannot be stated, can be more susceptible to topical blindness, and as a business placing emphasis on results-driven marketing content, the opportunity to overcome this almost always comes back to the data.

There are more unique searches being made in Google that historical searches, providing untapped new opportunity in content to cater for this, than with targeting all of the historically known searches combined.

Varying content types, encouraging wider team involvement, interviewing experts and generally trying new content origination tactics (whatever they may be) will keep things fresh and interesting for the creator and the reader alike.

Isolated content writers and marketing teams working separately from the teams dependant on the marketing content success will always limit the value a company gets back from the content being produced.

Teams working alone have little if any meaningful buy-in with the importance of the content they are making and tend to adapt a mindset of creating to deadline over creating for a purpose or end goal.

Ways in which you can easily identify this isolated working impact include the following:

- Missing evaluation of the impact that content is having
- No evidence of proactive content refinement after it goes live

- Primary focus on the content delivery date and words produced instead of sentiment towards content created
- Lack of feedback seeking, or any wins sharing

Isolated working is such an important and repeating characteristic of insufficient content for businesses that the following section sets out to resolve this issue.

Bridging and Integrating Mediums

There are many types of marketing platforms and mediums, and it still surprises me how many of them do the very best they can to work alone and in full neglect of everything else interacting with them regardless of invitation.

The more traditional marketing mediums can include print, direct mailshots, telemarketing, radio and television. The new norm of online mediums regularly include SEO, email/newsletter marketing, social media and forum-based marketing, Pay Per Click (PPC) advertising and others.

The intent of this section of the data-driven marketing content guide is to examine how some of these marketing mediums can working much closer together and consider a few of the added gains from doing so.

Internal Competition

It's strange to consider marketing mediums as competitors.

In fact, there should never be any justifiable logic to encourage two or more marketing mediums to compete over and above them interacting.

The origins of marketing mediums competing are often based on the need to battle it out for budget and retain budget once it is won. The same competition exists when you have fragmented teams, either fragmented by geographical location (for example, marketing teams in the United Kingdom, the United States, Australia and others) or by specialism (teams for SEO, PPC, public relations (PR), etc.).

Teams can become fragmented and isolated when team managers are tasked with growing their team and their portfolio under management, rather than contribution towards total company growth, and combined specialist team targets.

Any team involved with marketing content and results must have the same goal and objective understanding, plus the interdependency awareness of how each marketing medium impacts the other.

The ideal situation for marketing specialists is that data, insights and opportunities are shared. The limitations of one marketing medium proactively highlighted for the inclusion of another to sustain and improve it, the results obtained from one marketing medium fuelling the experimentation and growth of another.

Over the next few paragraphs, you can see the practical opportunities and gains that can be had through the successful integration of marketing mediums.

Online and Offline

One of the more puzzling practical integrations, but certainly something requiring thought and attention, is the integrated functionality of offline and online marketing content.

It is not uncommon for organisations to neglect effective tracking of offline marketing content completely, leaving it down to perceived foot flow and other objective-based decision-making to decide if something is working or not. For print mediums, it is easy to track sales/readership but less simplified to track how users are interacting between mediums, upselling or interacting with the brand from offline to online and vice versa.

People are relying on more touch points than they would traditionally, in no small part this is down to the ease of and volume of marketing messages and devices people are exposed to. This is also contributed to the technological advancements and self-servicing abilities of people to seek out information required, challenge, compare and contrast marketing content and make purchasing choices faster.

But online and offline marketing has the opportunity to do more than just tracking movement of people and purchasing decisions; it has the power to improve sales and build audiences.

New technology (for example, Google Beacons) provides hyperlocal audience tracking, engagement and content delivery.

This technology has been available for some time, but it wasn't until late 2018–early 2019 that it saw a resurgence in purpose and application.

An example of this online/offline integrated marketing content solution is as follows:

- Direct marketing mailshots are delivered within a 10-mile radius of a new store opening in the high street.
- Within the mailshot is a QR code, which people can scan using their mobile phone.
- The QR code provides the user with a discount code that is only operational for 7 days and requires them to walk into the store to claim the discount.
- Every time any person who has scanned the QR code, walks/drives/cycles within a mile radius of the shop, they receive an SMS text message.
- The message includes a countdown of the time remaining to claim the discount plus an update of the latest stock and most purchased items.
- The user walks into the shop, buys a product and the staff create a new account for them.
- The newly acquired customer now can be tracked each time they enter the site, reminded of previous purchases and advised of related product and common upsell opportunities specific to their buying behaviour.
- They are included in newsletter and email marketing updates, plus they receive and existing customer monthly mailshot through their door to update them about stock changes and new product ranges.

The previous example is a retail setting; however, the potential value of maximising the marketing content opportunity and impact through combining marketing mediums, as applicable to any business, just needs recognition of the potential and energy applied for setting up the integrated touch points and tracking.

Almost every retail outlet now seeks to capture email addresses at point of sale, send e-receipts and complete supplemental communications with easy new user generated by walking into and purchasing from their shop.

SEO Plus PPC

As someone who has worked in the SEO industry since the early 2000s, I've seen many amalgamations of SEO and PPC working together. From complete separation and encouraged competition between departments, right the way through to the same people delivering both services.

There is a genuine need for these two marketing specialisms to engage and actively interact, and it is this need which is covered in more detail now.

To confirm, the main difference between SEO and PPC advertising is fundamentally that all traffic coming from SEO (also referred to as Organic Search traffic) is free, whilst all traffic coming from PPC is paid for (you have to pay for every paid advertising advert click).

The other primary difference between SEO and PPC is the placement of the adverts within the search engines (SERPs). PPC ads are the revenue-generating element of search engines and therefore are always the most prominent advert types appearing.

Paid adverts (PPC ads) appear at the top of the search result pages (usually accounting for the top three to five adverts), marked with small 'ad' logos, whilst Organic ads take the remaining adverts and impact almost all other integrated search results, rich features and Google My Business result features.

Of the many reasons to integrated SEO and PPC are effectively for marketing content and wider business success, here are my top justifications:

(1) **Retail space.** If you are not optimising for both SEO and PPC, you will be missing out on 40% upwards of the potential clicks within the search engines that are dedicated to SEO and PPC advertising only. Just because you are not present does not mean that your completion are not. In fact, your absence would encourage increased competition levels through decreased bid completion and therefore lower CPC (cost per click) and CPA (cost per acquisition). The value of making the most out of the available retail space includes building your brand familiarity and awareness. Remember, even on paid advertising models in GoogleAds (formerly Google AdWords), you are only paying for the in-SERP adverts when they are clicked on (a different model to banner advertising and cost per impressions).

(2) **Combined data insights.** There are unique data insights only available from PPC, as well as those traditionally, primarily used by SEO experts. All of

these data individually are invaluable to business for marketing content (including adverts) creation, but when recombined, they lead to vastly improved opportunity. For example, Google provides AdWords, Keyword Planner and a host of paid data insights so that business can generate increased ROAS and invest more into paid ads. SEO experts use Google Search Console, Google Analytics, Google Trends, plus other free data tools and analytics. Mostly, these are concerned with how you are found, how you rank, the search queries people use, the changing trends, plus all of the post click user behaviour and interactions with your website. When combining these data you can identify keywords that are not feasible for PPC bidding due to high CPC and ROAS. These can be targeted by SEO for new marketing content building, plus helping to increase the sites quality score (therefore reducing the CPC). On the other hand, high competition, high volume terms which may take many months of authority building for page 1–3 SEO advancements can be bided on immediately through PPC. The data insights on the bidding (for example, the terms that led to enquires, the terms people clicked on, etc.) can help steer the SEO focus and prioritisation of topics, subtopics, informational content needs and lots more.

(3) **Increased data.** As PPC is instantaneous (the moment you have an active credit card and activate accounts, your adverts appear in preferred/paid for positions), you can gather practical data for improving adverts faster. It may takes days/weeks/months for SEO to generate the amount of data and marketing content information that PPC could (with the right budget) within a matter of hours. The information obtained related to advertorial CTR, key terms used, plus CRO all have potential marketing use for SEO and in wider content marketing efforts.

(4) **A/B testing.** We discussed previously about increased data use, and in part this also impacts the ability for increased experimentation and A/B testing. The testing should not stop at the advert, however, but filter through into dedicated landing page and CRO experiments, plus a lot more. The speed of PPC enables you to test and act on hypothesis, then use the data that become available to you for making wider website decisions and impacting all traffic landing on your website. For example, a PPC landing page can have a number of variations. This means you can alter headlines, button placement, messaging, short form use and other CTA (call to action) functions. You discover that version 3 of the PPC destination page works the best – this include a refined headline and supporting statement, a short form within the main banner of the page, plus a large green button with the wording 'continue' used. All of these items can be replicated to known similar pages (likely service landing pages and category level pages), positively impacting the value derived from all traffic (90% a combination of SEO and PPC) landing on your website.

(5) **Better results.** SEO and PPC are the perfect marriage. They overcome each other's weaknesses and collectively provide more returns than the sum of each of their individual component parts can offer. When SEO and PPC experts work together, they maximise the market share, act faster on new

trends, fuel one marketing channel actions from the insights of another and cost lower through authority building and topical business claim. The increased brand, product and service exposure increases awareness and trust, thus improving CTR and lowering CPA.

Practical Tip. Every time I work with a new PPC agency or in-house PPC team, one of the first things I work on with them is to experiment on opportunities for reducing paid spend on brand bidding and associated areas.

Brand PPC campaigns are often the most successful and largest paid campaigns within an account, but there is almost always paid spend waste on over brand bidding which can be scaled back, refined and left for SEO to pick up (for free).

There is no perfect, singular approach to testing this, it tends to be a case of incrementally reducing spend on brand terms within the account and closely monitoring SEO and PPC clicks and sales from brand terms until it reaches a point where there is a collective (SEO + PPC) total contribution drop. At this point, you know you need to increase the brand spend marginally as you have discovered the tipping point.

Whilst brand bidding is almost always cheaper with lower CPC values, the scale at which brand campaigns are pushed to perform means that you will be paying for traffic that could be free – something every business will want to know about and act upon.

Chatbots Fuelling Offline Interactions

Chatbot technology has been improving over the past few years to a point now where most people would not be able to tell they are conversing with a chatbot or a person via live chat.

Chatbots serve many functions, and a key one pertains to expediting the user journey from initial interaction to informed buying decision-making.

Whether it is a chatbot helping you find the most suitable pair of trainers for the Great South Run or using your informational cues to book a new car test drive, the potential for chatbots to fuel offline interactions is vast and steered by the effective delivery of information without relying on the user to find it.

Chatbots are only one example of conversational commerce, which businesses can seek out and explore for commercial advantage.

Social Media and PR Cycles

Encouraging social media experience-based user generated content creation and social media marketing can produce data and information ripe for PR, content promotion, user engagement and other cyclical approaches. This can be leveraged by effectively using new and existing users to build trust, confidence and expand brand exposure into new, relevant audiences.

Any experience-based industry has easy options to combine the efforts of social media with PR to maximise the results gathered.

As an example of this in action:

- A young couple go into a local restaurant driven by the poster in the window showing a 15% discount for anyone taking a picture of their food and sharing this on their social media channels (for example, Instagram, Twitter, Facebook).
- The couple are aged between 18 and 25 years and would naturally share content (especially visual content) anyway, so there is no aversion to doing so when incentivised.
- When the couple are led to their table, they see that each table has free Wi-Fi, plus a reminder to ask staff to snap them and share their photo for free on the company social media account.
- Once the couple are eating, they take a picture of their food, tag each other and the company in the social media post.
- They use the prerequisite hashtag detailed on the offer segment of the menu on their table.
- The restaurant updates its social media channels posts, responding to new engagement, including with the photo the new customers took, and asking them to leave a review.
- The restaurant also updates its business social media accounts by posting the photos that the couple agreed to have taken by staff when they were at the restaurant, and as the couple like the fact that brands are mentioning them in their posts, they share and engage with the posts as well.
- The restaurant's request for a Google My Business review is also accepted by the couple, and they leave a positive review.
- This review helps the local business appear in local search results as well as within voice-based mobile and home speaker search requests due to the increased trust and authority associated to them algorithmically from Google.
- More people discover them online, the review data get used to generate new PR content, more people begin to walk into the restaurant as they become aware of the brand and the cycle continues.

This is a simplified version of the many potential iterations that could exist within an effective social and PR approach, and hopefully this stems some actions with your own approaches.

In-Home Shopping and Online Ordering

AmazonFresh and Dash may be new names to many; however, this will not continue to be the case for long as they service two important consumer pain points:

(1) Convenience shopping for essentials. AmazonFresh provides early morning and same day delivery of many perishable goods and associated products

that people would traditionally 'pop-into' the local shop for, almost always with them paying a substantial premium.

(2) Shopping from your own home without the need to queue, log into online accounts, or complete any of the other timely actions which prevent fast buying on the move. Amazon Dash is a small electronic wand that enables you to swipe (scan) or speak directly into it, adding products to your AmazonFresh checkout process, seamlessly buying without any supplemental time-consuming actions.

This form of offline/online seamless buying and brand interaction is likely to be the future of consumerism, certainly for the younger demographics who will be brought up with the process in place, and see it as the standard approach to buy last minute products and increase the convenience aspect of convenience shopping.

Convenience shopping and merging online ease with offline availability doesn't stop here. Amazon continues to be at the forefront of this convenience revolution, another example of this in action being Amazon Locker.

Amazon Locker enables you to buy online and have your order delivered to a secure locker, removing the dilemma of only being able to buy and confirm orders at a date and time when you know you will be at home to collect.

This mitigates the annoyance of waiting around (often for the entire day due to delivery time ranges) by supplying unique locker codes for users and the provision of local lockers that are chose by the user at the time of purchase.

Amazon Locker is a fantastic way to see the way in which data-driven organisations are identifying and acting upon known audience pain points and then turning them into marketing and new business opportunities and differentiators from the competition.

This also demonstrates perfectly the integrated working of online and offline areas, plus the growth in marketing mediums, as they are extending into almost every part of our daily lives.

Emails and Workflows

Email as a marketing medium is one which most companies frequently use, but very few make the most of in an integrated fashion.

Emails can be the vehicle for marketing medium integration and play a vital role in many business workflows, leading, reinitiating, and progressing the user between other marketing mediums and steadily towards multiple end results.

A workflow can be defined as a repeatable process that moves people through the marketing channel in an automated way.

The key features of a marketing medium workflow include the following:

- Agile movement of people between marketing mediums
- Automated inclusion of people into a predefined marketing channel (of flow)
- Refined touch-points and personalisation of the user journey
- Frequent marketing contact with the audience

Chapter Summary

Three core concepts were discussed in this chapter: failed marketing content, practical ways to future-proof your business content, as well as integrating marketing mediums to maximise success.

As we progress into the next chapter you are supplied with application methods and approaches for targeted content build on key marketing channels:

- Search Engine Optimisation (SEO)
- Paid Advertising (PPC)
- Social Media
- Emails and Newsletters

Definitions

- Marketing medium: the way in which business can promote and engage with their audience. Examples of marketing mediums include radio, SEO, PPC, social media and more. Marketing vehicles are the specific component parts that get the marketing message from the medium to the end user. For example, radio is a marketing medium and the radio channel or station would be the marketing vehicle.
- Google Beacons: these are small battery-powered devices that are able to send one-way signals and interact with close range Bluetooth devices. Most commonly, the Bluetooth devices are smartphones and tablets. When businesses use Google Beacons, they are able to send location-targeted marketing content to people in the close vicinity (for example, a discount code to someone as they pass by a shop or a product promotion as a person walks down the aisle in the store with a latest offer).
- Hashtags (#): a form of social media metadata tag which is used on social networks like Twitter, Facebook and other socially driven services and platforms. The purpose of a # includes enabling users to apply fast, dynamic, and user-generated tagging so that it is easy for anyone to find messages with any given theme or content area. This helps discovery and engagement in topics faster as well as trend identification and inclusion.

Chapter 6

Creating Content for Marketing Channels

Marketing content is the focal point for success spanning all marketing channels. For every moment and monetary investment in marketing, the same degree of consideration needs accounting for business and marketing content.

In this chapter, we explore four marketing channels and the content approaches required to underpin success within each of them.

Before we drill down into effective bespoke content frameworks to the marketing channel, it's useful to delve into the supporting structures within any organisation required to facilitate successful content building regardless of the channel.

The first of these supporting structures is the content team.

The Content Team

Your content team is ultimately accountable for the ideation, creation and execution of all business content, regardless of purpose and intent.

The central roles within a successful content team include those below – these can be separate people, multiple staff or individuals fulfilling multiple functions:

- Content manager: resource planning, allocation, team management and service-level quality controller
- Strategist: aligning content needs, approach, tactics and outputs to goals, objectives and desired outcomes
- Writer: delivering the bulk of the textual content, researching and sourcing information
- Creative: producing mixed content types, positioning content visualisation and repurposing existing information
- Editor: extending the value, quality and correctness of content
- Coordinator: pulling everything together, tying actions into timelines and improving efficiencies
- Data analyst: supporting ideation, reviewing content value and reporting on success
- Promotion: building, understanding and nurturing the audience, pushing content out to the right people at the best times

Data-driven Marketing Content, 81–100
Copyright © 2019 by Emerald Publishing Limited
All rights of reproduction in any form reserved
doi:10.1108/978-1-78973-817-920191007

The Data-driven Ecosystem

As defined in Chapter 2:

'A data ecosystem is a collection of component parts created with a single collective purpose – to produce meaningful insights from data.'

The component parts of an effective data-driven ecosystem include the following elements:

- Analytics
- Infrastructure (IT)
- Machine learning, artificial intelligence and intelligent algorithms
- Applications

A data-driven ecosystem supports the historical, current, and future content delivery requirements for increased efficiencies and effectiveness when it comes to generating marketing content with repeatable results.

The Roadmap

Business marketing content cannot succeed without longer term practical strategic thinking, action plans and roadmaps.

Back in Chapter 4, this type of activity was defined as:

'A content action plan sets out and clearly defines the specific actions required to deliver on an end goal or objective area. Regardless of the objective the action plan provides the timeline of activities required to get to the desired outcome.'

It is the roadmap and action plan that tells the content team where they are at, where they need to be and how practically they are going to get there.

Every person and defined role within the content team understand how they impact the roadmap, items of expected shortfall, team and expertise capacity, plus any new role and expertise requirement.

The Promotional Plan

Leading us back to audience empathy, awareness, and understanding, content promotion keeps content writers' and creators' visibility and focus on the desired content applications and outcome.

The persistent function of the promotional aspect (including targeting, shareability and ease of promotion) helps multiple versions of the same content being built and ready (fit for purpose) for use throughout the delivery of a final campaign.

Examples of an effective marketing content promotional plan can include the following:

- Guidelines for brand messaging and measurement
- Clarification of audience personas being targeted
- Setting of expected promotion goals and objectives

- Creation of workflows and mechanisms for conversion
- Integrated action plans, dovetailing with existing content creation roadmaps
- Internal staff sentiment, support and buy-in
- External influencer surveying, social listening and interaction

The Content

Here is where the medium particular frameworks and approaches come into play.

Search Engine Optimisation

The right Search Engine Optimisation (SEO) content leverages data, turns potential visits into people landing on your website and nurtures every element of the information seeking and buying process.

When developing SEO content, removing purpose from the equation, the three key factors are trust, authority and expertise (EAT).

These three items need to be ever present as they are the foundations for contents ability to perform organically.

There are numerous page types for SEO; however, one of the most challenging for businesses to master is service landing pages – these form the focus for this part of the guide.

A service landing page is the destination for all of the users who you wish to fulfil a specific expertise area of intent. As an example of this, a digital marketing agency may have SEO as a service page, PPC, website design, etc.

The purpose of a service landing page is to provide search engines and users with all of the information, expertise, trust, authority and topical insights required for the page to rank highly.

For the visitors entering the website on this page, it is about enabling the user to convert without any unresolved barrier preventing them from doing so.

The challenge an SEO service page has (in fact, the challenge that all important SEO landing pages have) is this balance between servicing the user and serving the search engine.

Holistically, the answer is always to consider the user first; however, that is not always the case. For example, creating an amazing landing page about website development, with every user need fulfilled and question answered, that has unwittingly been excluded from search engines crawling or indexing the page, will fail to deliver any SEO gains regardless of the level of content value.

The framework to follow for an SEO service page is detailed next.

The 20-Step Checklist for SEO Service Page Content

(1) **Complete keyword research.** Establish a core set of terms, all within the same topic, and make sure that you have high-level (two words), mid-level (three to four words), and long-tail (5+ word) phrases covered. This will

ensure that you are working towards some of the highly competitive and longer timeframe terms expected to drive most traffic and conversions, without missing out on the shorter and medium timeframe terms which support that theme.

(2) **Create a URL structure that makes it easy for people and machines to understand and evaluate the page content.** Generally, URLs should be descriptive (without adjoining terms: and, if, then, the, etc.) and limited to three to five words. Service landing pages should include the service being mentioned and ideally a key qualifier – for example, 'https://www.example-domain-name/SEO-Agency-Solutions'.

(3) **Seed terms and variation.** Your core terms, synonyms and variations required factoring in when it comes to important page elements. This includes the title tag (which appears in your organic advert) and has some minor ranking value, the meta description (part two of your advert) which support CTR gains and relevancy, the h1 tag of your service page (marked up as a h1 tag within the HTML code) to reinforce relevancy to the advert and help reduce bounce rates and more.

(4) **Header tags.** The h1 tag establishes the primary theme of the page for users and search engines and in most cases should only be used once (there are arguments regarding HTML5 and multiple h1 tags, but in nearly all cases a single h1 tag is preferable). The remaining header tags (h1 through to h6) can be used multiple times, they reinforce the main theme and introduce subthemes, to show breath and depth of topical coverage. Effective header tag styling and usage can also provide clear page structure signals and encourage easy skim reading of content (even more so on mobile devices). In many cases an h1 tag can be supported with a subheading h2 tag, the latter filling the role or stating service differentiation and maintaining the website visitors' attention.

(5) **30–40 word introduction.** This sets the tone of the page, drives the user towards the desired outcome and (where appropriate) targets Google Rich Results including Google Answers. The introduction text should remove any informational barriers for the user and tell them what they are expected to do and why they need your service over the competitions.

(6) **Longer word counts.** Service landing pages can have complete content coverage and prioritised content ordering plus delivery to support deep content levels (frequently 2–3,000 word pages rank higher for longer) and content claim over all important subject matters relevant to the page. Approaches including tabulated content, accordion (expandable div coded) content and other tactics work well with getting deeper content text levels into a page without it feeling text heavy.

(7) **Mixed content types.** Unless your page is an Accelerated Mobile Page (AMP), that has been stripped of all time heavy components (images, video etc.), your page should be rich with alternative content types. Images and video content appear prolifically within integrated search engine results pages, and their inclusion helps with more visual users and conversions from other devices outside of desktop.

(8) **Supporting data.** Ideally you would use your own data and support it with industry trusted and publicly accessible statistics and insights when producing marketing content. These require updating over time (for example, every year when new research and white papers are created) and showcasing freshness of content and accuracy of information.

(9) **Call to action (CTA).** Every scroll needs to have a dedicated and targeted CTA. The easier it is for a person to taken action, the more micro and macro goals completions you will receive from your landing pages. A CTA could be anything from a clickable telephone link to watching a video or reading more content. CTAs should be based around guiding people through the buying journey as quickly as possible.

(10) **Testimonials and review ratings.** Company pages and service pages should have schema marked up testimonials and reviews. Schema.org supply the code to add to testimonials and review content, plus there are a number of external review providers who can support with generating and implementing this onto your website (you should only use testimonials and review schema appropriately (on relevant pages and not on mass or site wide) as there are Google penalties targeting spam use of schema). Reviews provide trust, reinforce expertise, and encourage herd mentality. Users trust customer reviews more than traditional word of mouth referrals and any unsubstantiated marketing claims.

(11) **Responsive by design.** All website content should have responsive design. This ensures that the content displays as intended regardless of device used to access it. All major CMS including WordPress have numerous responsive templates that can be adapted to suit business content delivery and design needs.

(12) **Internal links.** Linking related content passes authority and facilitates the aggregation and access to content all in one place. Service pages should limit the number of completing CTAs and internal links so that a user has the main focus of converting, over being distracted by other attention grabbing links; however, you need to balance this out with giving them access to information they may require to convert. A good example of this is a financial website giving access to legal information, terms and conditions, and other supplemental documentation include key features documents that they are duty bound to provide for the website visitor to make an informed choice.

(13) **Social proof.** Like testimonials and reviews for trust, social proof (think social media service-specific feeds and snippets from positive social posts) can encourage trust, buzz and interaction with the brand. Social PR is becoming an important part of the service selection process and provides quick and easy external justification for taking the next step towards service acquisition and buying.

(14) **Service features and benefits.** All of the traditional product positioning, features, benefits and associated informational areas require including in an SEO landing page the same as any other form of marketing content. They should be clear, concise and supported by fact, as opposed to

unsubstantiated marketing claims which can appear misleading or too good to be true.

(15) **Problem-solving.** People seek expertise and services because they have problems which they are looking for help with solving. FAQs, chatbots, live chat and other items can be effectively deployed into your service landing pages to give the user the comprehensive content support and audience attention needed. This broadness of coverage and placement of the audience needs first will always help service landing pages perform better online.

(16) **Name/Address/Phone number (NAP).** Another trust signal for the user as well as genuine business and entity signals for search engines. NAP gives confidence in the brand and enables people to act sooner.

(17) **Modifiers.** A modifier can be anything used to enhance a page. Often modifiers for SEO are referenced for items to prefix or append to title tags and headings to improve performance.
Common examples include:

- Adding an emotive term (for example, fantastic, amazing, best, memorable, etc.) to title tags
- Including a date to headings and title tags (for example, Best SEO Tips in 2019)
- Using numbers to entice clicks (for example, 10 best content ideas of 2019)

(18) **Reduce speed.** The faster content can load (consider mobile and desktop site speed as well as time to first byte (TTFB)), the fewer click loss you will see with people pogo sticking back to the search results before even getting to your landing page. There are many free tools to help with site speed including Pingdom and GTMetrix.

(19) **Accessible content.** W3C and Chrome developer tools provide free actionable insights for testing and improving content accessibility. This ensures cross browser compatibility as well as readability and content understanding for people with visual impediments (and using screen readers).

(20) **Increase content discovery.** Any SEO landing page must have external backlinks pointing to them. This facilitates referral traffic from relevant external entities and establishes trust and authority of the content being linked to. Highly linked to content from quality, topically relevant websites will outrank like for like competing sites with reduced backlink profiles.

Paid Advertising

A pay per click landing page can be the ideal destination to personalise marketing content, refine and experiment with conversion rate optimisation, plus pit the performance of multiple versions of the same page against each other to continually improve the value gleamed.

The framework for a PPC landing page is more simple that an SEO one – it's all about converting the user.

There are 10 main facets for the perfect PPC landing page which are covered next.

(1) **KISS.** 'Keep it simple, stupid'. Clean, concise and impactful messaging is paramount. Every item on a PPC landing page needs to focus on conversion, anything not aligned to that goal can be reduced in importance and often removed. You want to limit competing messaging, and calls t actions, so the user landing on the PPC page has clarity on what they are supposed to do, and enable that journey as quickly as possible. The human brain needs to be able to understand what it is looking at within fractions of seconds, so the less clutter and confusion on PPC destination pages, the better.

(2) **Prominent buttons.** CRO places heavy emphasis towards ease of conversion and obvious conversion choices. The more prominent the CTA buttons and short forms are, the faster people can identify and click on them. CTA buttons should be coloured separately to the main site colour scheme, and larger enough for easy mobile phone pressing (all touchpoints should be easy for finger and thumb presses). The text on the button matters (a lot), as does the size, shape and any button wording. These need to be A/B tested using Google Optimise or other webpage testing tools.

(3) **Think visually.** High-quality images and supporting video content can often stem faster decision-making. Imagery that is high quality and audience reflective can set the scene, reinforce professionalism, as well as trigger emotive reactions from users. Engagement can be increased with the use of images and visual content, plus people are accustomed to clicking, interacting and engaging with visual content, supporting increased CRO.

(4) **Trust signs.** Always need to be on place when you are expecting a person to convert. Star ratings, testimonials, case studies, associations, governing bodies, payment security and other areas can all be factored into PPC frameworks and landing page templates. This will help to convey safety signals that the user needs to overcome barriers to converting in single sessions, without the user needing to dig deeper on site or externally for landing pages and companies that do provide this security more effectively.

(5) **Page structure.** The positioning of every on page element needs to be hierarchically skewed towards conversion. At the top of the page you would expect a clear sales-driven headline, a supporting differentiator statement, buttons and clickable telephone numbers, plus a short form. The header section of the page would generally include a key business statement and prominent clickable telephone number.

As you scroll down, you would include evidence to back up differentiators, mixed image and video content, additional unique selling points (USPs), and snippets of testimonials, reviews and case studies (encouraging herd mentality and trust). Note: each scroll or segment would have a dedicated and specific CTA. Towards the lower section of the page you would consider removing information barriers that can prevent users from acting immediately.

Live chat, chatbots and answering of key front line and sales staff questions can all help with this. The base of the page can also provide supporting conversion opportunities including email and newsletter sign-ups, which can bring people into the marketing channel, but at lower emotive commitment levels. Remember, most people are also window shopping online, so capturing anything from them can be a win compared with having no potential to drive them into your marketing workflows.

The footer can also be used differently to any main site template. Removing unwanted extra navigational options, reinforcing social share, providing address information and more. You shouldn't take anything for granted with a PPC landing page; all template elements should be revised for maximum conversion potential.

(6) **Nurturing leads.** The addition of free guides, white papers and other sup-plemental value provisions on PPC pages have set and establish brand value as well as nurture people through the sales process in a less direct way. Incorporating multiple layers of conversion opportunities within your framework can help generate every ounce of potential from your paid marketing investment.

(7) **Event tracking.** You need to see every possible item within a PPC landing page as a trackable event that can be monitored and improved upon. From telephone clicks, and brochure downloads, to watching a video and clicking a social sharing button, you want to make every part of your PPC landing page trackable for testing and refinement. The mindset should be that every interaction had a value, and as a business you want to gather as much value from every PPC landing page as possible.

(8) **Advert reinforcement.** The largest challenge for PPC pages is stopping immediate bounces. The main driver for pogo sticking back to the search results is unexpected behaviour of the landing page. The landing page top of page (pre-scroll) information needs to align with the PPC adverts. Title tags can be reflected in the main heading, and supporting advert content (including the USPs that triggered clicks in the first place) prominently positioned in supporting statements and visible introduction messaging.

(9) **Divide and target.** Leads can be divided into three main areas (as detailed next), with each lead categorisation requiring unique support, information and associated converting options:

- Contact – Someone with the potential to become a lead, but at the moment they have limited knowledge on the topic or desire to act. They are not qualified to commit to buy at this point.
- Prospects – These are more established and informed than a contact, and a qualified lead. They have the motivation and budget to buy.
- Opportunity – Bottom of funnel, qualified prospect who is actively looking to buy and wants to feel empowered to do so.

(10) **Mobile ready.** Including responsive design, fast loading times and mobile friendliness. At a very minimum, PPC landing pages need to service a good mobile experience.

Social Media

Marketing content approaches and frameworks for social media, will, as you would expect, differ between platforms and social media marketing mediums. The social media audience of LinkedIn is very different to that of Facebook. Twitter as a microblogging platform has very distinct marketing content approaches to Quora.

In this case, we take Twitter and Quora for reference points and provide practical marketing content creation guidance for both.

Many of the specifics identified will have wider application to other social media outlets; however, it is important to have awareness of the nuances too.

Twitter

Developing content for Twitter as a business poses numerous challenges, not least because of the character restraints and limitations. This combined with the speed at which the microblogging platform trends and content intrigue changes, makes Twitter a relatively untapped marketing results driving medium for many small-to medium-sized business.

Twitter was founded in 2006, with an 80% mobile audience, and has grown to impact 100 million active monthly users and 500 million tweets per day (https://www.omnicoreagency.com/twitter-statistics/).

Here are the best practice content building items for Twitter that can help improve your business content. You will notice that some are direct content creation items, whilst others are more platform and approach targeting:

(1) **Hahstags (#).** A Twitter hashtag is any word or phrase that is prefixed by the hash (#) symbol. By adding a # prior to a relevant term and set of words, you are categorising the tweet and utilising inherent Twitter functionality for clicking or tapping on hashtags to view related topical content. This also enables easy trend inclusion as well as appearance in other notification and search operator functions and settings people opt in to follow. As a rule of thumb, all tweets should include a hashtag if they are intended for the wider Twitter audience. As a business, you should also make the most out of branded hashtags, associating the brand name to areas of topical interest.

(2) **Quick, frequent updates.** As a business you need to set expectations for Twitter covering fast and efficient content promotion, statements, information sharing and interactions. The Twitter ethos was established based on fast, simple communication, and that remains today. Twitter move quickly, as do topical interest areas and trends. What this means for creating content for Twitter is that you need to reference snippets from what

you have already written and be prepared to be reactive to new opportunities and interactions.

(3) **Twitter analytics.** Use the data within https://analytics.twitter.com to see the top mentions, top tweets, top followers and associated prioritisation information for new updates and repeat content items for repeat value leveraging. Twitter moves fast, but the things your audience digest and like to interact with, often remain consistent for longer timeframes. Vary your posts, track the data impact and adjust approaches accordingly.

(4) **Testing.** You will want to trial many things with your tweets. Time of day, frequency of tweeting and type of post (text only, text plus image, gif, etc.) will be good initial areas to experiment with. Something to keep in mind is that your audience will be growing and changing too, so 'known' insights will also require reverifying over time (quarterly works well).

(5) **Interaction over promotion.** Twitter should not be limited to a content promotion tool. If brand building and audience growth are your primary business goals from Twitter, I would apply the 80/20 rule to Twitter content; 80% of the time engaging and interacting with tweets, trends, question being asked and 20% of your Twitter content promoting your existing and new content.

(6) **Social listening.** Fifty percent of communication is listening. On Twitter, the listening aspect of marketing content is equally as important as the tweets and other post type updates. You can create Twitter alerts on your notification settings as well as follow trends and set notification updates. You need to be included in the business and industry conversations that matter most to you, so edit and refine these areas to proactively be included in the right conversations.

(7) **Building target Twitter Lists.** A Twitter List is a fantastic way to segment your audience into prospect groups and informational resources. In the same way that you can send people down different workflows and conversion funnels from other marketing niches, you can participate in bespoke marketing content and lead nurturing using Twitter Lists. Twitter Lists facilitate quick, effective targeting and grouping of likeminded people, with similar pain points and positioning within the information seeking and buying cycles.

(8) **Maximise characters.** When there are character restrictions in place (for Twitter this used to be 140 characters, and at the end of 2017 this was increased to 280 characters for many accounts), there is an opportunity to optimise each and every one of them for result-based gains. Consider Twitter posts as you would a paid advert. The elements to include are often the same:

- Leading statement/headline
- Emotive trigger to act – click/share/like, etc.
- Call to action

(9) **Social surveying.** You can gather informal and open surveys by asking a question or complete more defined and closed surveys through the use of

Twitter Polls. The purpose of this type of Twitter content is twofold. Firstly, you open communication channels to anyone following Twitter trends tied to keywords or hashtags used in your post. Secondly, you gather unique audience insights and direct business marketing data which can be used to improve current marketing content, grow your social following and impart company expertise form brand building and more.

(10) **Templating the brand.** You can reinforce the brand through the hashtags used and branding on visuals. This should not be over the top and obvious, but subtle and encouraging of increased brand research and discovery, should the Twitter community decide to take the communications further. Logos on images and other brand-based visuals can increase the value derived from your content efforts.

(11) **Answering questions.** Solving problems and answering questions can be fantastic exposure opportunities for businesses. Ideally, your experts would have active business Twitter profiles and be provided with a framework from which they are able to quickly engage on Twitter, knowing what they can and cannot say.

(12) **Direct messaging (DM).** DM can be used for damage limitation (for example, public expressions of dissatisfaction and complaints), as well as for nurturing people trough the buying cycle. As a company you can request people to follow you to DM them and steer the conversation closer towards more meaningful and deeper (non-character-restricted) conversations. DM can be used as per closed audience email conversation and to drive telephone communication, trial and content downloads, plus other items including meeting scheduling and more.

(13) **@mentions.** When people become increasingly aware of your brand plus the main experts inside your company, they will begin to mention you directly within tweets using the @example-profile-name mention functionality. Mentions should be dealt with as a priority over other scheduled updates as these are effectively active audience members waiting from reply. There tend to be more customer service requirements with @mentions too, so combining fast replies and frame-worked approaches with direct messaging can be important.

(14) **Integrating tweet CTAs.** Twitter and other social media mediums need to be seen as an integral part of all your content efforts. Embedding Twitter CTAs (actual 'click to tweet' embedded code for easy Twitter single click posts for people reading and interacting with your content) will increase the social reach of your business content. Including key statements and opinions within content that visually stands out is a great means to increase perceived blog post quality, and push the content and the brand out to wider audiences.

(15) **Audience selection.** The ability to find, follow and name check influencers in your marketplace means that as a business you can cultivate the audience you desire in Twitter. The trap businesses regularly fall into with social media marketing is the numbers game; the more impressions and clicks, the better. This is actually a false positive. Twitter is about targeted content

marketing, placing the best and most relevant content in front of the most influential and ready-to-engage audience as possible, as frequently as you can. You can look to ego-bait people with pre-release access to guides and mentioning them in tweets. You are able to encourage reciprocal 'follows' by identifying and following the key players (non-competing people) in your market. Other tactics for audience selection and nurturing include requesting opinion, expert statements and feedback from people to start the conversation.

(16) **Retweeting with comments.** It can be all too easy to get retweet heavy handed and find yourself sharing all types of content with the hope of building your audience. Try to avoid this as it begins to feel spammy and can undermine your genuine efforts to become accepted within key Twitter communities. Instead, use the retweet with comment functionality and add something meaningful to the conversation and the content promotion. Adding opinion when retweeting content helps with the credibility and likely engagement of other people to your retweets over the original content sharers' posts.

(17) **Trending topics.** You can view all trending topics on Twitter, as well as set the interest areas more pertinent to your business. By being trend active and jumping onto new, relevant trends (relevancy can be location as well as service, industry and solution based), you place your experts into the conversations generating most interest and exposure at any given time.

(18) **Community focus.** A mindset over an action, but something which you should take to heart. The Twitter community is just that, a community environment. As a business, you have to consider the type of content and interactions completed. Consider Twitter as a fast access to your community, plus an opportunity to share, discover and immerse yourself in your community. Twitter users are a social media and commercially savvy group, so treat them as such and support them through credible content updates and short communication exchanges.

(19) **Bio completeness.** The business and key staff business Twitter bios should be seen as a top-level reflection of the organisation. Branding, key messaging, CTAs, and contact information should be consistent, optimised and managed. You need to factor in this consistency with all social media mediums too, as this can also increase brand awareness, SEO gains (name, address, phone (NAP)) and wider control over marketing messaging.

Quora

Quora is an open forum question and answer (QandA)-driven community (social media platform and online platform), where experts share insights, ask for information and opinion, and collaborate. Originally opened in 2010 through beta mode, Quora was initiated by two ex-Facebook employees and targets expertise and knowledge sharing.

Community sentiment on Quora can be assessed by upvoting and downvoting replies plus the direct sentiment shared through commenting functionality, which drives the QandA characteristics of this platform.

Quora can be seen as a question and answer search engine (almost a combination of Google as a search engine, Wikipedia as a community content-building forum and LinkedIn combined with Twitter for the professional community as well as actively engaged audience).

There are similarities between Quora and other social media mediums (including Twitter mentioned previously) including:

- Bio completeness and consistency
- Topical engagement opportunities and trend awareness
- Mention awareness and interactions

There are also Quora-specific marketing content nuances to take note of too, with the key ones detailed now.

(1) **Quora spaces.** A new feature on Quora that functions similarly to LinkedIn groups and Twitter Lists. Spaces are collections or community groups based around shared interests. You can follow Spaces to have them appear within your feed and prioritise target groups most valuable to your marketing content efforts.

(2) **Add question.** The primary push element of Quora. This gives you the ability to target individuals and groups of people on Quora privately or publicly, requesting information, insight and direct answers to questions posed. You have a main headline (usually in the form of a question), followed by supplemental statements, context and details. You can also include information links, integrating the post with your website and other content including extra social media platforms.

(3) **Share link.** If you have created a new research paper, interactive content guide or other content form which you wish to gather genuine feedback on, the 'share link' feature can be a useful tool. It is important to include a comment with this, steering feedback, setting context and driving the community towards a useful business and marketing outcome. As with all social media shares, avoid misuse, spam and other low-quality pitching within features like this. You will find that engaged and informed audiences like those on Quora quickly become disenchanted with this type of thing and publicly call out unwanted spam posting.

(4) **Request feedback/answer.** When you pose a new question, a great feature of Quora is that you can request a number of specific people get asked to answer it. You can prioritise this based on frequency and recency of answers plus other factors including number of followers and topically related answers supplied.

(5) **Quora pitch.** The tonality and pitch of answers you provide should be considered as trusted, authoritative and informed. The information given

needs to be unique and not simply a re-hash of blog content, or a link fuelled reply pushing people to read your feedback elsewhere. Quora as a community likes opinions and expertise sharing, and I would consider Quora to be a place to interact with your peers and reinforce credibility. Most industries have key influencers and thought leaders with active Quora profiles.

(6) **The community is the editor.** If you post something that undermines the posting guidelines, or simply falls woefully short on insight, value or expertise, the community will downvote and actively quash it. Your marketing content on Quora needs to be expertise based and value adding. Quality is the foundation of business growth on Quora, something that you should always keep to the fore.

(7) **Integrating other social networking sites.** When getting started with Quora (as per other social media mediums) you can fast track your audience exposure by adding Facebook and Twitter friends and followers to your Quora feed. Frequent problem-solving and active community involvement will help expand your marketing content reach.

(8) **Private messaging.** Like Twitter and Facebook, Quora also provides private messaging functionality for any Quora connections (aka Twitter followers). This can be used in the same manner as the direct messaging facility previously described for Twitter.

(9) **Thought leadership.** This combined with trust and expertise reinforcement is the primary goal of Quora. You can drive referral traffic to your website, build relevant links, promote content and gather data (on top of many other impact areas), but essentially you are growing the visibility on expertise and thought leadership. As Quora questions and answers can appear in the Google SERPs, you can also help increase solution-based impressions and brand visibility.

Emails and Newsletters

Email and newsletter marketing content can quickly become dated, unresponsive from an audience perspective and repeatedly fail to deliver on commercial expectations.

Email and newsletter marketing efforts can soon lead to diminishing returns as once set up, and automated in many cases, the content and approach loses its personalisation and traverses into the pitfall of treating the recipients as numbers instead of individuals.

There are many metrics for concluding email and newsletter success (CTR, open rates, website visits and more), plus a host of free and paid for email automation, management and analytics packages to monitor and refine them.

Developing marketing and business content that works within the requirements of email and newsletter success parameters though can be more challenging, and ultimately increased awareness and a more thorough consideration of the best practices that impact this can help revisit and revive your approach to emails and newsletter marketing.

Emails

Emails can form the staple marketing content medium delivering a steady flow of leads throughout seasonal change, troughs and peak interest trends and other changeable factors in your marketplace.

The following framework demonstrates the main characteristics supporting successful results-based email marketing content. I am making an assumption that you have email analytics in place to test and refine everything (from headline and greeting, to time of day, internal email linking, CTAs and more), and as such the focus is on the content of the email communication itself.

(1) **Sender (from label).** Taken for granted by many companies, but the person sending the email is one of the fastest exclusion (deletion, spam filtering) characteristics that people use. Emails should come from the company (brand) and a relevant person (ideally) or team expected to send email communication. Even if you use external agencies to promote content, you should consider granting them access to a branded email account.

(2) **The greeting.** Email clients like Outlook give the user the option to see various email content prior to opening the message. The initial greeting (the first few words on the first line of an email communication) is one of them. The greeting used conveys relationship, intent, qualification of communication and other perceptions including quality of the message. The greeting used needs to be professional, personable, concise, and meaningful. Not easy for 10–20 words, but important to get right.

(3) **The headline.** Every word in an email headline must serve a purpose. Effective headlines entice email opens, establish the relationship between the sender and the recipient and demonstrate relevancy plus personalisation. Also referred to as the subject line, the good headline tells the story in as few words as possible and answers the 'what's in it for me' question that generally encourages people to click.

(4) **Body text.** Emails should adhere to strict quality guidelines and deliver a consistent framework which any repeat recipient of your company emails can recognise even with the removal of any branding. Emails are notorious for spelling and grammar mistakes, incorrect styling, poor functionality and unexpected operability issues. Whether you decide to include images, quotes, embedded content or other component parts within your emails, it doesn't matter providing they work, operate as intended, and don't undermine the quality of the communication. The speed of email messaging can lead to hurried updates and unwanted thin value information sharing. The quality of body content within emails can even become a differentiating factor due to the myriad of lower quality competing examples users get exposed to on a daily (often hourly) basis.

(5) **Start with a summary.** Put the important information first. People are unforgiving when it comes to their email attention span, so say the most pertinent points first, and then back them up later in the email (ideally with links to website content). An effective summary (think executive summary)

relays the key details as quickly as possible. Remember a summary doesn't need to be repetitive of content shared later in the email; moreover, it should have stand-alone content value.

(6) **Goal orientated.** Each email sent should have a single purpose, and you need to tell the user what that is. The goal of the email will drive the CTA used, the pitch of the content and the brevity of the communication. If you want people to buy something, the email should be constructed around this isolated end goal. Typically, this would include a discount/promotional code, product imagery, review and testimonial snippets, product differentiators and much more. If the email does not deliver on the goal, do not be tempted to dilute the goal, or move the goal posts, refine it to improve the objective-based outcomes you intended the email to fulfil.

(7) **Bullets.** To assist brevity your email should maximise content styling and display (bullet points a great example of this in action) to make the most out of every character and line break in the body of your message. Readability and skim reading are fundamentals for the accessibility of communication when it comes to emails.

(8) **Responsiveness.** All emails need to be fully functional for design and content covering every device, Internet speed and email client used. Part of this should include speed of content delivery, mobile friendliness and associated items.

(9) **Closing statement.** Ending the email is almost as important as opening it. The closing statement covers a similar role to that of the opening statement (summary) and is responsible for closing the deal. If the reader has got to the end of your email they are ready to act, but they still require persuasion and specific guidance. Closing off an email tends to be lazy and ubiquitous, rather than compelling and emotive. Master the closing statement and see your response rates, clicks (and other intended email events) progress past historical benchmarks set.

(10) **Visuals.** Images, gifs, video and other visualisations appeal to the more visually driven recipients, whilst segmenting content and reinforcing context to the more textually natured people. Increasing numbers of people require visual triggers to respond to email messaging, even more so when using mobile devices to read messages.

(11) **CTAs.** Call to actions is likely the one area companies test along with headlines the most frequently for email content. Ensure your emails include consistently motivated CTAs (for example, the intended outcome is to download a form, read a blog post or buy an item – they should all be geared towards one outcome as opposed to many), non-competing or excessive demands for the user attention, easy clickable (and 'pressable') events and actions, at least one CTA per attention area on the email, plus mixed content types CTAs.

(12) **Structure.** Content structure, formatting and design should follow that of a PPC landing page in many areas. People have a familiarity with reading and do not want to be challenged to question-anticipated email content layout, structure and design elements. Headings have expected parent and

child relationships; images have standard integrations within body text; lists should be introduced and main heading, subheadings, and straplines separated by font, size and positioning on the page.

(13) **Unsubscribe.** There are a number of GDPR and subscription best practice to consider for email communication, an 'unsubscribe' link is one of them. You need to make it simple for people to self-qualify and unqualify themselves from your marketing lists. This means you are working with data that have integrity, and people who you can confidently assume are interested in what you have to say. Don't undermine or skew metrics by limiting the accuracy or credibility of your data, they serve no useful business purpose.

(14) **Alt text.** Don't overlook image alt text when you create and send email communications. A large amount of the people reading your emails will not display images by default (in Outlook, for example, by default you need to right-click and select display images). This means that the placeholder image boxes will need to have well thought out and descriptive content to lead the reader to take action and opt to view all images.

(15) **Signatures.** A signature in the email should in most cases reflect the standard company branding and messaging for consistency of approach, but they can be more than that. If your business has won awards, is a member of key trusted associations and governing bodies or has exciting announcements to make, the email signature can showcase them. Related links to topically relevant news, articles, blog posts and guides can also work as micro goal completions and traceable events, assisting to capture the users' attention when the main email content may have failed to do so and to help facilitate further reading and service interest of the user on the subject matter.

(16) **Tracking.** Every event of an email content needs to be tracked. UTM tracking code can be added to all clickable parts of the email message including text links, images, video content and other embedded resources. If you want the user to do something, you need to place UTM tracking code on it. From this code you can track all the email events through Google Analytics and tie in email marketing content success with wider marketing channels and mediums. You will also be able to assess how email marketing content is assisting other types of conversions and how it is contributing towards total marketing success.

(17) **Follow-ups.** Rarely will a single phase of emails be enough. There is a lot of competing noise within email clients, and most of the time (regardless of testing) you will be emailing someone at the same time as many others. An effective email follow-up communication will do one of the following three things:

- Prompt the removal request from a passive email recipient who has no intention to migrating into the active lead status, thus helping qualify the remaining target audience

- Drive event completion as they finally have what they needed to convert on some level
- Initiate contact – Often for further information, clarity on areas the email does not effectively redress, or movement of communication to the recipients preferred communication channel

As email communication and business content contained within emails are so widely poor in delivery, there are a couple of important things to avoid as well.

Firstly, don't overuse the functionality provided. Just because you can capitalise everything, mark the email as high priority, request read receipts, add emoticons, plus include a whole host of other feature-based things doesn't mean that you should. Keep things simple. Test one refinement at a time. If there is no valid reason to include something, then leave it out.

Also, techniques can get dated and spammy fast. Use the data and constantly text several email templates all the time. Adding a postscript (PS) to the end of an email may have been the deal maker three years ago, but how many times has a PS strapline caught your attention recently for the right reasons?

Finally, avoid attaching supplemental information to emails unless they have been requested or are prerequisites for the contact. Attachments will result in blocked messages, excessive file sizes and unwanted distractions for the end user.

Newsletters

Excluding the shared best practice that exists between email and electronic (email delivered) newsletter content, the following are newsletter-centric factors to improve your approach. You should include all of the previous email framework advice in your newsletters by default.

The distinguishing intent for a newsletter that separates it from email content purpose is that a newsletter is meant to inform, educate and nurture your existing audience.

Successful newsletters maintain a consistently high level of open rates and action completion.

By choosing the right content and approach to newsletter marketing content, you keep prospects in the buying cycle, showcase company growth, expertise and new product or service ranges.

You can guide readers to digest cornerstone content that reinforces your brand as the trusted experts in the industry, as well as encourage them to take part in company events, exhibitions and other audience knowledge and value-sharing exercises.

Newsletters can also be effective internal sentiment and marketing communication tools, helping retain staff, reinforce consistent marketing messaging and share company success including new business acquisition.

For the purposes of this framework, however, the attention is on external audience newsletters as these are generally the business priority.

Characteristics of effective newsletters that you can factor into your approach include the following items:

(1) **Consistency of delivery.** A newsletter should be scheduled in advance, consistently included as part of your business marketing calendar and sent the same day of month and time of day. A newsletter delivery can be considered in the same light as a newspaper delivery. People are habitual by nature and encouraging people to habitually receive, read and take action with your newsletter inspires increased, consistent results.

(2) **Creativity and novelty factor.** Newsletters enable you to show personality, put faces to brands and have fun with your audience. Creativity and novelty value do not need to be seen as low-quality triggers; in fact, getting this right can skyrocket engagement, brand value and wider audience sentiment. The correct novelty application reinforces that you understand your audience and can connect with them on extra humanistic areas outside of simply price, positioning and other traditional marketing pitching.

(3) **Setting expectations.** Newsletters take longer to read, skim through and digest. As such you need to be clear from the outset how long you expect to take up of a person's time (especially when this is the first newsletter they receive), how much is covered, supply quick link access to all important information, and give the user alternative content types (as opposed to emails, PDF attachment can work well).

(4) **Limiting self-promotion.** This can be one of the hardest things for marketing teams to master, as it feels counterintuitive, but newsletters are not the place to push sales messaging (leave that for emails). Successful newsletters always have something new, interesting and credible to say. They passively sell to the audience through showcasing trust, expertise and latest topical news. Ninety percent of a newsletter needs to be brand neutral. Let the stories and the people speak for themselves.

(5) **Company and community crowdsourcing.** The newsletter needs to reflect you people in the company as much as it does the target audience. When ideating the next newsletter, include as part of your process asking the wider company for any charity work they are doing, local event they are involved with, expertise and industry changes they are aware of, new business and case studies that can be used and other useful qualitative data gathering. You can also ask your audience questions about what they want to read about, what they like about the current newsletters and any suggestions they may have for improving them.

(6) **Integrated team and collaborative working.** As a thread throughout this practical content guide, collaboration is key. The more you can integrate and share examples of data, team and insight integration, the increased chances there are of applying a multiplier effect.

Chapter Summary

The focus of this chapter is bolstering your ability to create marketing medium-targeted content that is driven by frameworks and approaches proven to increase results.

An effective content team underpins all the content you produce, and the important roles and structure of a successful content team have been covered in some detail.

Individual emphasis and content delivery best practice was supplied for distinct marketing mediums:

- SEO
- PPC
- Social media; Quora, Twitter
- Email
- Newsletters

Definitions

- UTM tracking code: a small piece of code that you can attach to any URL, providing you with the functionality to track a source, medium and other details (like a campaign name). This enables you through Google Analytics, to identify where searches came from and analyse, benchmark and improve the effectiveness of marketing campaigns.
- Ego-bait: this is the process of approaching key people, thought leaders and influencers with the application of servicing their ego to get to an end result. An example of this in action includes requesting people to read and share your content ('if they like it') based on 'a great recent article of theirs you have read'. Ego-baiting techniques are great for increasing response rates to content promotion and generating expert quotes, feedback and information for new content creation.
- Quora: as defined earlier in this chapter, this is an open forum question and answer (QandA)-driven community (social media platform and online platform), where experts share insights, ask for information and opinion, and collaborate.
- Crowdsourcing: this is the gathering of information, ideas and feedback (including reviews and sentiment) from a group of people. This can be incentivised with products, payment or other perceived value sharing or free (the incentive being inclusion, expertise awareness or general wish to participate).
- Multiplier effect: the increased final outcome from combining two or more distinct entities. In the context of this chapter, a multiplier effect refers to the added value derived from combining disparate data sets and/or isolated/distinct specialism (like SEO and PPC).

Chapter 7

Overcoming Content Barriers

There are many reasons why your business content is failing to deliver on expectations, and most companies outside of the superbrands are all feeling the same pressure to generate greater results from the content they create.

In Chapter 5, attention was placed on defining the 10 fundamental reasons why content fails (a reminder is next), plus mechanisms were supplied to help future proof and protect your marketing content from dwindling returns:

(1) Insufficient planning
(2) Strategic shortfalls
(3) Absent storytelling
(4) Internal emphasis
(5) Ineffective conversion mechanisms
(6) Overlooking SEO
(7) Budget
(8) Mispositioning
(9) Content promotion
(10) Quality

Chapter 6 introduced bespoke frameworks and approaches for producing marketing content that works, dedicated to the marketing channel in question.

Now it's time to overcome some of the most challenging marketing content applications, namely result effective content for:

- Websites
- Ecommerce sites and stores
- Mobile devices
- Voice and screenless search

Content for Websites

Company websites can accomplish many things, fulfil numerous roles and deliver a myriad of functions for businesses when the content is right.

Data-driven Marketing Content, 101–118
Copyright © 2019 by Emerald Publishing Limited
All rights of reproduction in any form reserved
doi:10.1108/978-1-78973-817-920191008

A website is not simply a marketing brochure or information resource.

When nurtured correctly, a website can be your chief business generation and fulfilment tool, a customer support, awareness and interaction platform, plus a sales and logistics vehicle – and that's just for starters.

Website capabilities are only limited by the people ideating, implementing, maintaining and advancing them, not by the opportunity they provide.

When it comes to developing marketing content for websites, there are a few significant basics to consider.

EAT. Expertise, authority, trustworthiness. Whatever purpose the page has for the content to enable the user to act, or search engines to consider the content rankworthy, it needs to be EAT driven. EAT is about credibility, showing it on a page and reinforcing it with as many other signals (link qualifications, inclusion of governing bodies, awards, backlinks and more) as you can. Simply telling people you're an authority is not enough, it needs to be backed up by evidence.

YMOYL. Paying extra attention to pages which are deemed 'your money or your life' require higher standards setting. YMOYL pages are those that as seen having greater perceived impact on your well-being. From financials and safety to physical well-being, these pages need to be treated differently. There is added emphasis on the expertise and authority demonstrated on these page types.

Purposeful. No content should be implemented on your website without a clear purpose. You need to be asking yourself:

- Who is expected to read/share/interact with the content?
- What is the expected user outcome?
- What benchmarks is the content expected to achieve?
- What external content is this competing against?

Web-ready. Content that is written for the web is not the same as any other form of content writing. Web copy and creative content is skim read and scanned, it is not thoroughly digested or read in its entirety. All web content has a fundamental requirement to load fast, be responsive on all devices, Internet speeds and browsers, plus accessible to all people regardless of any impairments (including visual limitations).

Fast tracked. Most website content is read on mobile devices, frequently when people are on the move, and with highly limited attention spans or the readers' ability to dedicate focus. Your content has to reflect this; make content segmented; showcase the core points of the content and make it easy to bookmark, share and download information. Everything you want the user to do needs to be accelerated.

Say the important things first. Everything you need the website visitor to look at and know about must be provided as high up on the page as possible. Every scroll will reduce the amount of visibility on your content. Calls to action, trust signals, unique selling points, topical reinforcement, brand differentiation, all need placing as high on the page as you can.

Reinforce expectations. The largest loss of traffic occurs within the first 0–3 seconds that your page loads, and the people landing on your site decided whether the page, content, brand they are seeing matches the expectations they had when they clicked on an advert (in most cases, more than 80% of website traffic comes from SEO and PPC combined). The keywords used, quality of your images and content, plus the topical relevancy, all impact this.

Consider data-driven behaviour. Don't fall into the trap of being different for the sake of being different. Use your data to tell you where people click, see heatmaps of what they focus on and understand the related content they need to digest to convert. Then use this to reinforce and ease their movement and flow through your site towards the intended outcomes.

Snippets. Most pages on websites can benefit from the inclusion of short content sharing or snippets. These tend to be in the form of information widgets (think about quotes, short summaries of case studies, social media posts, tickets, reviews and more). Any concise methods that you can deploy to enrich the breadth and depth of coverage and value on your web pages should be considered until they detract from the end goals.

Keyword selection. The types of keywords you use in your website marketing content require as much consideration as those selected on paid advertising. Keyword research plays a more prominent role in website copy than in almost all other marketing areas. Intelligent use of high volume terms and supporting those with short-medium term competitive keywords will assist natural ranking of your content, and the behaviour of the people searching for products, services and information in the first place.

Speak to your users. Use real-world language in your web copy. This helps provide a personable tone and style which can be trusted and easy to associate with. Take a look at reviews and other qualitative data sets to get a genuine feel for your audience terms and nuances and look to reflect them in your content. Google, Search Console, Keyword Planner, and Trends are perfect places to look for this, as can competitor website testimonials and case studies (plus external review sites). In Chapter 5, we discussed understanding your audience, this has direct application here.

Add extra headings. Content needs to be broken up. Paragraphs for web copy should be short sentences, and within the body content you can use bold and other tactics to help content (salient points) stand out. Well-written headlines facilitate content skim reading and the understanding of page content without the barrier of excessive reading needs. Successful subheadings can support people sharing content and converting without them reading 90% of the web page copy.

Mixed content. No web page should exclude images as a basic need. The adage 'a picture paints a thousand words' is true with website copy. People need to be able to understand content quickly, take action immediately and get on with all of the other distractions life poses. Image and video content (plus other content types like infographics) can provide informational reinforcement and get people to their end destination sooner.

Test everything. Data must fuel your website content decisions. From headlines and CTAs through to button placement and advert text, don't make assumptions, use the data instead. Google Optimise is a free way to A/B, split and multivariant test things on your website without the need for any developer skills (something discussed in previous chapters in some detail).

Takeaways. When you know the purpose of each page, you can be clear and specific about what the key takeaways are for the user. Look to limit takeaways to a single theme and no more than a couple of key points. Ensure expected take-aways are seeded throughout the page and in mixed content types (some people are visually driven). As a minimum the main points and associated CTAs need including at the start, middle and end of your web page copy.

Assume people know nothing. Information gaps and low-savvy searchers create large visitor and conversion losses. Recue any jargon, and define important points. You can include the frequently asked questions at the base of pages and do lot more to educate, inform and nurture your audience, as opposed to isolate them. This does not mean dumbing down content, it is about making content inclusive and demonstrating an awareness of your audience needs.

Use lists. Leading back to easy content digestion as well as supporting inclusion on items like Google Answers (Rich Results), ordered and unordered HTML lists help search engines and users understand and act on your content sooner. Anything that is process driven, a defined number of steps or able to be summarised, should be included in bulleted lists.

Benefit orientated. Website content relies on benefits to make things happen. If there is no gain to be had for the user, the likelihood of them volunteering anything benefit free is minimal. If you want someone to download a brochure, they need a perceived benefit for doing so. The same applies for form completions, product purchasing or other events. Benefits need to be emphasised on above features (a common mistake marketing copy fails to overcome).

Tabs. Tabulated (or tabbed) content means that the same visual retail space can be used to cover multiple content areas and subject matters. While from a traditional SEO stance, invisible/hidden content will not derive the same value that visible content will by default, for mobile search and the value of completeness of topical coverage, tabs can be a useful web marketing content tactic.

Tables. HTML-responsive tables are a useful way to separate content and group details into logical content displays for websites. Table content also has the potential for including within Google Rich Results notably when the search intent relates to comparison themes.

Data and stats. Every claim and statement needs to be substantiated and backed up by data. You need to lift your content from being assumption and claim based to credible and authoritative (think about the EAT point covered earlier).

Remove waffle. Marketers are renowned for excessive words and waffle. Apply an objective waffle filter to everything you include and implement on your website. The use of lists, tables, and snippets will help with this.

Be consistent. Brand messaging, tone and style support brand associated beyond your website. A company ought to have detailed brand guidelines that anyone producing website (or any other marketing business content) can adhere to. This (consistency of approach) consolidates the brand purpose, positioning and messaging regardless of the individual creating the content. Content consistency also provides a more seamless journey through your website and other marketing mediums which all integrate as part of the buying funnel.

Collaborative community. A person landing on your website for the first time needs to feel reassured that they are in the right place and feel like they are part of your community. At a basic level, this is fulfilled with the right words, sentiment and imagery (covered previously), at a deeper level this includes feedback mechanisms, supporting herd mentality, data-based refinements and SMART updates.

Content for Ecommerce Sites and Stores

Ecommerce sites (online stores) pose some of the most difficult challenges for business and marketing content creation.

Getting the balance right between CRO/selling and authority/informative content provision is a real issue and one which changes based on type of page (category, product, company, etc.) and other variants.

Another content obstacle is granting the user access to all the details required to make an informed purchase whilst making the buying process as fast as possible.

These and other problems are solved in a practical way next with the use of Ecommerce content cheat sheets (frameworks).

Ecommerce Content Cheat Sheets

The main characteristics for effective ecommerce marketing content at the category level are listed now (with the product level information following directly after).

For an ecommerce shop, the category page is second in priority, with only the home page having a greater impact on site and marketing content success.

While the focus here is on two ecommerce content types (category and product pages), it is necessary to cater for a much broader set of content provision to raise the perceived value of the website, through its content, substantially higher.

The content-rich areas of an ecommerce site should include (and not be restricted to) news, blogs, research papers, guides, FAQs, case studies, videos, images and much more (for example, interactive content and additional visual content like infographics) (Fig. 7.1).

Content for Ecommerce Category Pages

(1) **Logo.** The brand image that links back to the home page site wide.
(2) **Call to action, contact details.** The brand differentiator/strapline plus clickable telephone number.

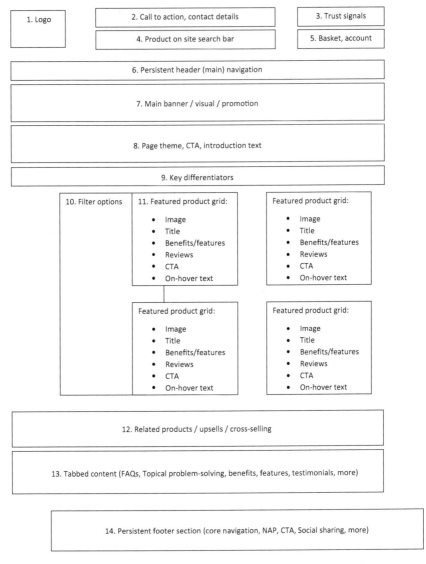

Fig. 7.1.   Ecommerce Content Cheat Sheet – Category Page.

(3) **Trust signals.** Company star/review ratings, often accompanied with company social media sharing buttons. The use of web and industry standard symbols (for items like basket, etc.) is common as most online shop traffic will be coming from mobile devices.

(4) **Product on site search bar.** Within website product and information search facility, enabling any page product discovery.

(5) **Basket, account login.** The main actions you want website visitors to complete. This doesn't have to be reduced to just these two areas; however, usually this would exceed five options.

(6) **Persistent header (main) navigation.** Access to the category level, and top performing product level filters for static landing pages on the site. This would also include sales and other evergreen content.

(7) **Main banner/visual/promotion.** The visual and CSS (Cascading Style Sheets) overlay (search engine friendly and readable) prominent theme and purpose of the page. Usually, this would incorporate the main header (h1 tag) of the page plus the initial subheading (h2) as the supporting statement and main call to action.

(8) **Page theme, CTA, introduction text.** The content that reinforces expectations and benefits, and drives the user to click into product level content or make a purchase. The use of 'Read more' expandable div (CSS) content delivery can enable you to substantially increase the content levels and user worth from this section of the page without pushing product information lower (unless the user decides they need to read more to take purchase action).

(9) **Key differentiators.** These can be benefit and feature based, specific to the category, or wider consistent brand and marketing messaging (for example, free postage, next day delivery, etc.).

(10) **Filter options.** The likely canonical child (see definitions at the end of this chapter if you are unsure of what canonical refers to) page variations of the main category and section-related product level selection options. This enables the user to drill down into the product area faster.

(11) **Featured product grid (items) or subcategory areas.** This helps the business to decide which product areas to highlight and encourage the website visitor to buy. The items included tend to be those of high interest and ROI.

(12) **Related products/upsells/cross-selling.** Anything which can push average order values, transactions and basket volumes up. For the user, this supports purchase completeness (for example, some items require accessories to work), and for the business, this facilitates single-stop shopping and greater sales per visit/user.

(13) **Tabbed content.** By enabling tabs of content, the web page is able to use the same amount of pixel/visible space for delivering numerous volumes of extra content. This content is readable by search engines, supporting SEO value, but often (especially on desktop search) delivers reduced content ranking gains for SEO (the exception being mobile search where this type of content delivery and clickable user behaviour is expected). The types of content coverage can vary and should reflect what your audience needs to make buying decisions. Frequently, this would include question and answer content, reviews, case studies, testimonials, deeper information about benefits and features. Tabbed content can also be a useful place to incorporate blog articles, news content, research papers, guides and other content types (like video) that you want to give the user access to without distracting them from buying.

(14) **Persistent footer section.** This serves many functions. A company name, address and phone number give added trust, as do company registration details link to important company level pages (about, contact us, mission statement, environmental policies, Ts&Cs) and the primary categories of the website. The footer can be the place to capture micro goal completions (those leading to contact or a sale) including newsletter sign-up, brochure downloads and associated action and event triggers.

(15) **F-shaped content.** People scan ecommerce pages in an 'F' shape according to long-standing eye tracking research (see more at https://www.nngroup.-com/articles/f-shaped-pattern-reading-web-content/) – this also holds true for mobile devices.

For easy site structure and content positioning understanding, and general usability, you will most likely want to include a persistent breadcrumb navigation which is marked up with schema.org code.

Other factors to consider at category level include the following.

- **Content pagination.** This is the page ordering of a series of pages so the user can skip through ranges faster and search engines can understand what the primary and ranking page is.
- **View-all content.** Expediting the time required and the clicks needed to see all the products and filter options relevant to the category in a single place (and one click).
- **Extra schema.org mark up.** For example, aggregate offer code (note: schema.org code is HTML code which helps search engines understand and therefore attribute value and rank content types, a full list of scheme and structured data mark up can be seen at https://schema.org/).
- **Internal links.** Links from other pages and content types on your website pointing to categories to help steer the user to important sale areas of the site, and pass internal topical authority and ranking signals (including the topics and terms the pages are intended to rank for) serving to improve the perceived importance and hierarchy of these categories within the total site overview.
- **URL structure.** These should include the primary keywords, be concise and intuitive for the user and search engines.
- **Metadata.** The adverts that should appear in Organic Search (providing they are deemed relevant to the content and well written) combining title tag and meta description. This requires keyword and trend data insights, core term inclusion, CTAs and other factors. Primarily Organic metadata need to be as relevant, unique and tailored to the user as possible, enticing them to click and delivering the expected journey from SERP to site.
- **Brand exposure.** If you have award-winning products, have received recent media coverage or as a company win awards, adding this below sub filters and product grids can be the final trust and authority signal needed to make someone buy.

- **Product application.** Practically showing the use of products will support people visualising the products in their life and lead them to emotionally attach themselves to the products sooner. This tactic is encouraging quicker buying habits and reducing price point and other product comparison barriers.
- **Keyword selection.** There are many ways to discover what category level keywords you need to focus on. Internal to your business, you can use Google Search Console, Keyword Planner, Google AdWords insights and Trends data. Externally, you can use Amazon search bar suggestions, Google-related search suggestions, competitor analysis and high-volume ranking sites like Wikipedia for inspiration.
- **External authority.** Through link building and category promotion (consider influencer marketing, product reviews, new product launches), external trust signals and ranking authority (as well as referral traffic) can be passed onto the category pages on your ecommerce store. The more you can optimise these pages (site speed, technical performance, internal links, external links, core terms seeding, etc.), the easier it will become to land people onto the core pages of your site and covert people faster and more frequently.
- **Frequent updates.** Query deserves freshness, and related Google algorithmic factors contribute to how prominently category pages will appear in search engines. By using the new data sets you have in GSC, GA and other areas (refer back to Chapter 3), you have constant opportunities to refine, refresh and improve your content. This will benefit staying on top of search trends and audience behaviour changes.
- **Glossary and jargon busters.** A fantastic way to remove information barriers to purchases and increase the range of terms that category pages are associated to for the major search engines.

Content for Product Pages

As you would expect for a consistent journey provision, most of the characteristics of a category level ecommerce framework are also present at product level.

There is the addition of a product comparison table (point 10 in Fig. 7.2) which caters for granular transactional information for final product selection.

Other than that, the nuances include product visuals and product level data including product details/benefits and features.

Added trust signals are included within the same visual segment as the product details.

You would expect a product page to appear differently to a category page as the primary purpose is different (Fig. 7.2).

A product page has a small set of purposes; selling the specific product, upselling/cross-selling to related products and getting people to commit to buy.

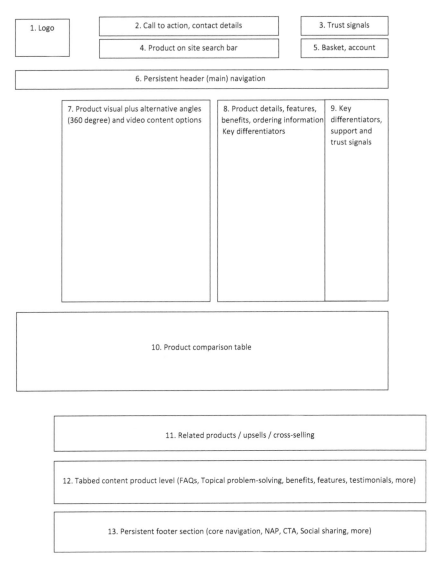

Fig. 7.2.   Ecommerce Content Cheat Sheet – Product Page.

Other important considerations for product-level marketing and business content include the following:

- Descriptive and summarised content
- Social sharing
- Mobile ready and fully functional

- Unique content (not scraped, copied, or manufacturer content)
- Delivery information (free, next day)
- Product reviews
- Amazing product descriptions
- Use of 'power words' that evoke emotion in the reader
- Use of 'action words' to stimulate user events/purchases
- Remember to tell a story (benefits/value)
- Comparison content
- Page titles, URLs, headings are all important (equally as the category level)

Content for Mobile Devices

Mobile traffic contributes to more traffic than any other device, surpassing desktop over the past few years in most industries.

Google made the 'mobile first' move in 2018, prioritising mobile content over any other form (traditionally desktop) of content delivery within their search engine.

At the time of providing this practical business guide, there is no single more important content delivery type to get right for marketing team and companies, than mobile – after all how many people do you know who doesn't own and keep on them at all times, a smartphone?

Mobile continues to provide one of the biggest business barriers to marketing content success, but this doesn't have to be the case.

When considering the role of marketing and business content for mobiles, you need to contemplate the access of the content and the user-friendliness of it. There are also very clear mobile behaviourisms to factor into the mix.

The features unique to mobile content creation and delivery are detailed next, and the 'mobile content cheat sheet' with the approach provided is based on a typical category/service level page on a website (Fig. 7.3).

(1) Logo – Responsive to screen size and clickable site wide to the home page
(2) Clickable Tel – For easy contact from any page
(3) Buttons (login/social) – Three to five clickable buttons that provide access to the most important company pages and social business syndication
(4) 'Burger' symbol navigation, plus key site categories – Single click access to top-level navigation, then clickable through to sub navigation
(5) Search bar – Full content and product/service search throughout the website
(6) Breadcrumb navigation – Easy supporting navigation for the user and increased understanding of where is the website hierarchy they are currently placed
(7) Pre-scroll primary content (text) – The core messaging, page theme and user-driving information

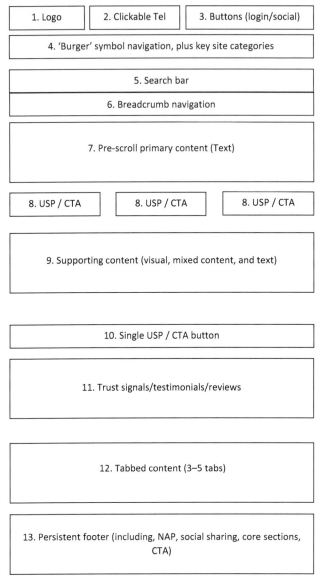

Fig. 7.3.   Mobile Content Cheat Sheet.

(8) Multiple USPs/CTAs – Generally three, but you can use a second segment of these. They tell the user why they need to act now, and/or facilitate the click

(9) Supporting content (visual, mixed content and text) – Deeper content removing barriers towards conversion and building mixed content value

(10) Single USP/CTA button – Reinforcing the main intended user event from the page
(11) Trust signals/testimonials/reviews – User-generated content, supporting herd mentality and solving trust gaps
(12) Tabbed content (three to five tabs) – Everything else the page needs to give the user to educate, nurture, inform and guide them towards a desired outcome. This fulfils the comprehensiveness of topic/product/service coverage required for SEO, the user and business needs
(13) Persistent footer (including, NAP, social sharing, core sections, CTA) – The final chance for conversion as well as trust and engagement capturing

There are added mobile centric factors to take note of when it comes to approach and delivery of marketing content. The main areas are covered now.

Content ordering. The top to bottom of page content delivery matters a lot. The same as with traditional 'above the fold' marketing content approaches (now 'pre-scroll'), the most important content needs to be provided first. The content ordering has to lead users through their first contact with the page through to their intended outcome. Repeat users need to convert faster than new users to the site, brand and product/service; however, you need effective content ordering mechanisms for all users throughout the buying cycle.

Headline importance. The content triggers that stand out more on mobile viewing (not just headlines) have an added importance, requiring additional though, keyword research and testing for mobile. A mobile user can be expected to understand and act on solely consuming headline information (as in many case, through effective skim reading your readers/visitors will do just that).

Mixed content. It almost without stating that mobile content is more visual and interactive than desktop and other content types. By nature, people look to press things on mobile devices, they have been taught that this is the expected behaviour and will quickly become disenchanted if they cannot click most of the page content. Video inclusion is common practice for overcoming information barriers and educating people on a topic. A video is expected to be short (up to 3 minutes max) and broken down into a series if the topic requires longer attention.

Image quality. It is expected to be higher for mobile users than those on desktop. Primarily, this comes back to the mobile audience and their familiarity plus added importance placed on the content type. Businesses also up their game with imagery on apps and mobile devices, so this raises the benchmarks, and you need to act on this.

Mobile first mindset. All business and marketing content needs to be developed for mobile use first, and all other use (content digestion and delivery) second. Eighty percent or more of your website traffic and sales will come from search engines, and they are (Google leading the way from 2018 for mobile first indexing) mobile content prioritised. If you are still producing content for desktop first, this needs to change. Reverse engineering and shoe-horning desktop content into a mobile framework don't work as it not the optimum mindset or approach to take. This will also be restricting longer term success with your wider business culture towards content creation regardless of intended use.

Burgers (hamburgers). These are the three horizon lines that make up a clickable item, replacing the fully listed main navigation that is present on almost all desktop variations of a website. A burger symbol is the expected 'click to view symbol' for users on mobiles and smartphones to see the main navigation without the visual impact that a fully displayed navigation has on mobile devices.

Purpose impacts length. There is no single word count that works best (although for core service pages that normally rank higher are 2,000–3,000 words from data-backed experience). Added to this, the page purpose will directly impact the required department and word counts for content delivery. A white paper, cornerstone content page or information hub may have 10,000 words on the topic divided between several pages. A product may have 500 words on a page. The important fact here is to understand the purpose of the page and reflect this in the content coverage you provide. Earlier in this topic, we covered the use of accordion (expandable div) content delivery, tabs and other ways to delivery the same potential content levels without the negative visual impact.

Optimise forms. As well as other expected conversion items, forms cannot be expected to function the same for mobile as they do for desktop. Mobile users are predominantly 'on the move' and therefore have a fraction of the time, attention levels, or motivation to spend time completing forms. Reduce the fields, remove unnecessary information, ensure they are responsive and mobile friendly. You can also make forms into two or three stages for completion on mobile if there is a requirement for added user details. This helps set expectations and facilitates easier mobile form completion.

Short content. Mobile content should not be short content in terms of number of words or value derived. With responsive design templates the new norm for website design and online entities, there is no valid justification not to create deep, comprehensive, best of bred content for mobile the same as you would for desktop and other outputs. The presentation of content, ordering and interactions will change (consider expandable divs, tabbed content and other areas previously covered), but the quality has to have the same aspirational quality. Having stated this, paragraphs, segments and sentences need to be shorted in how they are presented on mobile devices. This is directly based on screen size, usability and readability.

Remove pop-ups. In many ways pop-ups have limited use as standard on desktop content delivery too; however, even more so for mobile devices, a pop-up is an unwanted annoyance and distraction that should be removed for mobile devices. The added difficulty of touchpoints on mobiles and the limited attention span of the user rule these out for mobile use. You need to remove any form of intrusive interstitials from your mobile content.

Modular design. Think about the mobile framework as a screen made up of small and distinct modules (or cards/placeholders). This facilitates snippets of key information being presented and encourages topical completeness, without the impact on look and feel.

Mobile behaviour. The way the user acts on mobile devices is very different to any other device. You can refer to Google Analytics (and Page Analytics) data and other data sources including Google Optimise, heatmaps and others to base content decisions on meaningful data sets. Don't assume anything; people will not behave as you want them to, as you do or as might be the most efficient traits. Take a look at the content paths and funnels users take on mobile and compare/ contrast this to desktop and tablet behaviour. Mobile users will have unique pain points, content discovery needs and very limited time or patience – this will all become visible through the clicks and associated data you have access to.

Mobile streamlining. If there is a single takeaway of note with mobile content delivery and creation, it is streamlining for mobile. Always keep this in mind and ask yourself 'how can I make the user experience easier?' Scrolling pages instead of pagination are one practical example of this in action, another is modular-based content inclusion described previously (Fig. 7.3).

Content for Voice/Screenless Search

Over the next five years, voice search will double the size of user searches, and your business wants to be voice and screenless search capable as soon as possible.

To put voice search into context, it is the technologically driven marketing and business change equal to mobile phones and smartphones. Consider the rapid adaption of domestic users for voice assistants (think about Amazon Echo or Google Home devices).

In the same pattern, we have seen with mobile overtaking and solidifying its position as the dominant search device over desktop in the past decade, we are now starting to see the initial signs of voice and screenless search, extending its intent as the next transition from mobile to voice.

Screenless search is not the same as voice search (voice search optimisation or VSO), as it includes other non-screen mediums including Virtual Reality (VR). Much of the screenless search optimisation opportunity, however, sits with voice search and VSO, which is why this has been the predominant focus in this guide.

As a marketing team, professional, copyrighter or wider corporate role and business entity, you have a duty to become screenless search ready and embrace the opportunity that voice search provides.

Some people maintain the stance that voice search is and will continue to be fundamentally informational; however, there has been substantial growth of m-commerce and conversational commerce, demonstrating that increasingly people like to participate in online shopping on the move.

Here are 10 ways to maximise your content and optimise it for voice and screenless search.

(1) **Larger quantities of lower volume search query targeting.** Getting your content to rank and appear for voice-based queries requires longer-tail keywords identification and targeting replicating the conversational element of spoken rather than text queries.

(2) **New search trends.** Voice search has led to knew search trends including growth in demand for content catering to 'near me/near by' 'close by', and other location intent items.

(3) **Mobile growth.** Mobile has surpassed desktop, fuelled by home assistants/ voice-activated speakers, wearable technology adaption, plus continued mobile and smartphone user bases. Due to this, traditional mobile content development and mobile optimisation (as detailed earlier in this chapter) requires including more prominently in voice and screenless search content building.

(4) **Location, location, location.** Increases in 'on the move' search has led to greater needs for location intent targeting. Location destination pages, and other local content creation, link building, and general local buzz around your content, will help discoverability of your content for voice. This is based on the added perceived importance of location as a ranking signal tied to understanding the context and intention of voice-activated search.

(5) **Storytelling.** Storytelling has always been most engaging within a verbal supportive medium. The voice search growth has encouraged content to tell more stories, and people to digest greater levels of voice content. This can be seen in the resurgence of podcasts and webinars. Both offering business and marketers to capture new brand exposure and interact with wider audiences. Content can be refreshed, added to and repurposed for extra mediums based on audio demand.

(6) **More precise content.** Voice queries often have very specific intended outcomes and in most cases are closed answer queries. As an example of this 'where is the nearest café?', 'what does SEO mean?' and 'Who is the president of America'. There are explicit ways for content to target these queries as well as make a valid claim for inclusion within the Google Answers and other Rich Results (Featured Snippets), which provide high CTR gains plus added in-SERP brand exposure. Currently, Google Home and Assistant rely on Featured Snippets (the websites that are ranked in the 'pre-results' or 'position zero') and are therefore appearing as a Featured Snippet. You can gage the business value in this because of the fact that more people than ever are focussing on how to rank for and optimise content to appease Featured Snippets. A few of the main tactics include:

- Short (25–35 word) definitions high up on page content
- Bulleted lists
- Table content
- Extract match question and answer content provision
- Structured data mark up (on relevant items including author, recipe, address and more)

(7) **Action and event based.** There are many home assistant actions and events which account for large proportions of query groups. Content can be built specifically to focus on this growing need with the use of content lists, number bullet points, schema.org mark up and more. Actions can include many things including recipe reading, direction provision, event times and much more.

(8) **Immediacy.** For voice and screenless search, users almost always have 'right now' requirements, only searching for information at the point of which

they need to take action and make final decisions. For example, 'What café serves vegan food?' and 'What time does the co-op close'.

(9) **Natural Language Processing (NLP).** Covered in part with the long-tail search query targeting, but express to people, NLP includes awareness of conversational patterns, terms and distinctions like regionality. User-generated content and other audience reflective tactics work well here.

(10) **Citations.** Google My Business, Bing Places, and other niche, plus industry-related external sites are needed to reinforce the location, brand and genuine entity signals for the search engines, as well as helping individual discover your business. Due to the location motivation for voice search, these types of supporting local signals are required for high ranking and therefore inclusion within the highest-ranked content referenced by mobile devices and home assistants to return results.

For some added screenless search insights, here's some ways to optimise for VR as a business.

VR encompasses all the elements a person needs to compensate for when considering the 'try before you buy' mentality.

In situations where it is problematic to hold, touch or see important information (consider buying a second property overseas), VR can solve many of the questions by placing the user within the environment. It can also expedite the time required to compare numerous alternatives without added time demands placed on the individual.

As a practical application of VR with marketing content, Google created 'VR view' so people and businesses can embed 360-degree videos into the content websites and the traditional video marketing tactics still apply, including:

• Web-ready file sizes
• Contextualised and theme supportive text
• Logical, keyword inclusive and descriptive file name and description
• Optimised embedded code and structured data (schema.org) for search engine understanding
• Optimised title tags
• Web-ready hosting options (YouTube plus domain embed)
• VR transcripts
• Social sharing, PR and related promotion
• VR content time (<1 minute in many cases)

Chapter Summary

The goal of this chapter was to overcome some of the most prolifically challenging content areas for business namely content for:

• Websites
• Ecommerce sites/stores
• Mobile devices
• Voice and screenless search

Frameworks have been provided for consistent and repeatable content production and templated use. These have also been supported with detailed approach considerations to follow.

The next chapter takes a look at your existing marketing content for business, explicitly actions you can take to make it work harder and provide greater results.

Definitions

- Canonical tag: coded as 'rel canonical', this tag tells search engines that there is a preferred or master version of a page. Canonical tags can pass authority to another page, or be self-referencing to clarify which page is the canonical version.
- Power words: terms that are used to encourage emotion with the user and help important content (like product descriptions) stand out from other competing attention content. Examples include extra, thrilling and rich.
- Action words: often used to support CTA, an action word has an intended purpose to drive the user towards an event (or action). Examples include begin, go, jump.
- Schema.org: the collaborative community which provides code (schemas) for structuring data on the Internet. Schema code helps search engines understand content types (for example, reviews, address, recipes and more), enabling the content to appear in Google Rich Results (Answers, Carousels, more) and other applications.
- Featured Snippet: also referred to as a pre-result, position zero and rich result. A Featured Snippet is an in-SERP Google item that sits above the standard set of results, often fuelling home assistance and voice-based search queries. Featured Snippets tend to have above average CTR due to the placement of them above other competing SERP results and the activation including voice search.

Chapter 8

Making Your Content Work Harder

Eighty percent of the marketing content performance opportunity exists within the content you have already produced, currently failing to deliver on its ultimate contribution towards your marketing and business goals.

Hundreds of hours and thousands of pounds (a conservative guestimate) have been invested into ideating, creating, editing, implementing and marketing the content you have decided has a role for your business.

In one way or another, the vast majority of this content is housed on your website, engages with your websites or is processed through your website.

In this section of the business guide to data-driven marketing content, the overriding objective is to qualify your actions for improving your business content and making it work harder for contributing to its true result potential.

Due in no small part to the time and budget demands of many competing facets within your organisation, most (if not all) business content receives one initial chance to succeed, placing itself on the 'revisit and refine' radar when it does work, or (as in most cases) it fails to deliver any impact, thus adding itself to the nonperforming bulk of content that disappointed to deliver.

Consider Your Website as an Iceberg

The tip of this iceberg peaks out above the waves, representing the home page, contact us, about us and 10–15 core: company, service, solutions, and/or category pages on your website.

Bobbling below the surface, with intermittent and unexpected visibility include a small proportion of hero (cornerstone or evergreen) content pages. These have surprised and captured traction with your audience: a hub page, community section, white paper, guide, infographic, blog post, new article, interactive content item, or other video, image or content type that outperforms all expectations.

Then visualise 40 times the mass of the visible and semi-visible content dragging the iceberg under the water. The hundreds of pages of content rarely being seen, and accidentally or incidentally being found, causing limited, if any, awareness, excitement or contribution to the peak of the iceberg everyone interacts with and enjoys.

Data-driven Marketing Content, 119–132
Copyright © 2019 by Emerald Publishing Limited
All rights of reproduction in any form reserved
doi:10.1108/978-1-78973-817-920191009

This submerged bulk weighs down the tip, slows momentum, reduces visibility of the whole and gets added to more frequently than any other part of the iceberg.

Now, think about your website and where most of your content goes.

Each content entity you add to your website impacts the total site health, performance, trust, speed, functionality and authority.

Every piece of content is either growing the proportion of high impact pages on your website, or pulling the top performing content down, reducing result benchmarks and slowing the total site success.

Irrespective of the percentage divide between the top-performing content and the remainder of your website underperformers, your content can work harder, and it all starts with revitalising your existing content.

Revitalising Existing Content

One of the common marketing content frustrations is that after all of the effort placed on creating content, the business end result fails to deliver on expectations.

Poor business content performance can create a negative internal sentiment towards content writers and designers, plus reduced spend, with increased justification for future content building and budget allocation.

This type of company culture keeps the content underperforming and supports a negative cycle which needs to change.

The fastest and most effective way to increase your website content results is by revisiting your existing website copy and making it work harder towards your business goals and objectives.

The following points will all help achieve this.

Refreshing data. Google (and other search engines) use Query Deserves Freshness (QDF) as part of the algorithm for deciding the value of content tied to the newness of it. By revisiting older content (6 months old or more), the freshness alone will support better results. By adding new data and quotes (including external facing links to new related and noncompeting content on other websites), you can validate the content relevancy through its refresh, helping it to rank higher in Organic Search and extend the lifespan of content. This approach can be part of the monthly activities for your content and marketing experts, to keep momentum going.

Re-pitching articles. Through Google Search Console (GSC), you can identify the search queries your content is ranking for and has appeared for over the past 16 months. Using these data, you can see how search behaviour has changed and refocus content to make it rank higher for the common terms and higher volume search queries. Tactics for optimising content through refreshing it include adding/seeding identified terms and variations in:

- Page title tag (small ranking factor and relevancy signal)
- Meta description (for relevancy and CTR gains)
- Main page header/h1 tag (reinforcing the theme and sending topic/term intent to search engines)

- Initial/pre-scroll introduction text (to reflect to the user they are on the right page and help reduce bounce rates)
- Subheadings/h2–h6 tags (supporting main term variation plus feeding main topical relevancy)
- Body text (non-spanning, relevant term reinforcement)

Re-promoting content. Add some paid budget behind the content that you know (from looking at behaviour flow in GA and assisted conversion paths) supports end results. Do the same for content that had initial high impact but has since tailed off performance wise. Build remarketing lists for paid advertising and embark on some paid social media advertising. Use small amounts of marketing budget to experiment on paid content promotion and incorporate this into your ongoing marketing creation process.

Feature targeting. In the Google search engines, there are many Rich Results and integrated search features that can be effectively targeted to increase impressions, traffic and ultimately returns from existing content. Each of these Rich Features has specific ways to revise existing content and help claim them for your business. In Chapter 7, some tactics were shared to directly impact inclusion in Google Answers (one example of Rich Results) – here's a summary of this:

- Short (25–35 word) definitions high up on page content
- Bulleted lists
- Table content
- Extract match question and answer content provision
- Structured data mark up (on relevant items including author, recipe, address and more)

Improving shareability. Social PR can help with the buzz, engagement, shares and backlinks your content generates. Social sharing CTAs, easy social share facilitation and general application of tactics to increase shares (placement of sharing buttons, skim readable content, Tweet to share call outs in the body text and more) will improve the content reach and traffic. Including Open Graph tags on relevant content will enable you to control the content provided when people click on the share buttons, amplifying the impact of shares and controlling the content messaging.

Updating dates. There tend to be lots of chances to build date-specific content (for example, 'The 10 Best SEO Tips for 2019'), and these have limited lifespan, directly attributed to the date of the content. By updating the content with insights and changing the date to the current (or next) year, you can quickly keep content active whilst targeting the new date-centric search opportunity. It is these types of quick actions that become a positive working habit within organisations, supporting systematically greater content gains.

Maximising internal links. Internal links are the way in which you sculpt your website hierarchy, telling the search engines what content is most important and steering people through link functionality to other internal pages. Internal links pass authority and can be used for noncommercial content to increase the value and ranking success of commercial content. Blogs, guides, articles and other content types frequently have fewer compliance and other restraints meaning that they can gather increased social shares, external backlink authority and traffic – all of which can be passed on to the main converting pages on your website.

Revise headings. Updating the main heading and title tag to reflect latest search data and broader industry trends (using GSC, GS and Google Trends information) helps improve CTR, bounce rates, plus potentially average ranking too. One of the reasons why existing content has the potential to return the best and quickest results is that you have all the data to act on at your disposal, plus the content is already indexed, has some level of authority, and just requires some added focus and care to grow the gains derived.

Building backlinks. As internal links support the passing of internal (same site) authority, external backlinks provide the external trust and authority signals (plus referral traffic) to your website as an entity and to individual content items, plus topic areas. Backlinks are the external votes of confidence that tell Google and other search engines the content exists, is credible and is an authoritative destination for the topic in question. Re-promoting existing content; repurposing quotes, data and insights for new link volumes and socially sharing content on business accounts for fresh engagement signals will all encourage increased metric performance gains. I've seen many situations where the main factor missing from content success was lack of external trust signals.

Improving usability. The main focus for nearly all content and marketing teams surrounds landing more people onto your website. This approach leads to excessive audience waste and limited user engagement or satisfaction. There is also a disproportionate amount of expertise and focus related to increasing the value received from all of those extra visitors. Ninety to ninety-five percent of all visits to a website fail to provide any immediate company gain through conversions. This means that for every hundred people visiting your website today, you are only directly gaining from 5 to 10 of them (5 being most common). Improving site speed, responsive design, ease of reading, intuitive content rendering and other factors (shorter forms, consistent site template, easy to use navigation) all help with content and site usability, and ultimately conversion rates for contact and sales.

Creating series. Lots of websites have related content that can be re-purposed into a series of pieces, each extending the lifespan of the content within the associated group. Series work fantastically well for driving repeat users back to your website and maintaining contact with your audience. They can also help with content expectation setting and repeatability of social promotion.

Developing content hubs. Content hubs are basically the grouping of topically associated content that is disparate at present (usually blog posts, articles and news items dotted all over the site) into one deeper, richer content resource. Usually content hub sits at the root level of the website to demonstrate the evergreen intention of the information and the expected importance of the topic to the audience. I've worked on many marketing and business content projects where revitalising website copy by combining thinner content levels and lower value articles delivers end results much greater than the sum of the component parts.

Fix errors. Broken and inaccessible content will not deliver any company marketing results. Content frequently gets blocked from appearing in search engines in error and deleted from websites without any consideration of the contribution it is making to business success. 404s, 410s and 5xx (500, 510, etc.) header status pages need to be reviewed for the historical value they have provided, and reconsidered for activating and improving, rather than deleting. Through GSC, you can see pages/content blocked by your robots.txt file (the most common unwanted mistake in blocking content from search engines), as well as those with on page (in code) meta robots blocks too. As a business, you should lock down CMS access so that only a couple of key staff can delete content, and that needs to follow a specified process which will include items like traffic, impressions, backlinks, event completions and other areas. Other on page broken content needs to be factored into this also: items like missing alt text, broken links, and broken images.

Improve quality. Quality is not a static measurement. Looking back over the past 15 plus years in SEO, marketing and digital, I know wholeheartedly that the level of content quality as a benchmark today is substantially higher than at any other time working in the industry. As an example of this, blog posts five years ago were lucky to exceed 250 words and were extremely keyword heavy, with very limited reflection of expertise, opinion or other standalone value. Go forward five years, and blogs can be some of the most visually appealing, data led, interactive content pieces imaginable. It is rare to see successful businesses omitting to invest heavily in best of breed website content. To improve website content quality, you should audit the site in its entirety. To do this, simply create an Excel file (ideally as a Google document), with the headings including word count, last update date, readability (1–10 score), usability (1–10 score), errors (free field cell to detail what errors, so they can be fixed), spelling/grammar issues, and yes/no fields for items like images, video, subheadings, related reading and social sharing. The value of a Google doc for this is the shareability, so that you can specify and track the people needed to carry out the task and to process drive it for consistency. This type of website audit can be segmented into monthly actions, but it is useful at least annually to complete a full audit. This means that you can benchmark and improve on content, plus have defined start and end dates to mark the project (or phase of the project) off as complete.

Revisit URL structures. Blogs, news articles and other content types auto-populate URLs through the CMS by default. This leads to long, unwieldy and complex URL structures that are difficult for users to read quickly (reducing CTR) and challenging for search engines to understand (reducing ranking gains). It is important to go back through your CMS and update URLs so that they are:

- Keyword inclusive
- Concise
- Intuitive

- Easy to read
- Relevant
- Trend reflective

Add structured data. It is important look into ways in which you can increase the context and understanding of your content and create frameworks for systematically ensuring this is adhered to for all content created. Context and understanding can directly improve your content ranking in search engines (notably Google). We have covered Schema.org in previous chapters, and I strongly suggest an initial action implanting this code on all relevant areas (in a non-spammy fashion – i.e. only for relevant content).

Increase content depth. Use the data you have at your disposal to understand the pain points the content you have provided solves, and then increase the depth of the content coverage to cater for added standalone value and contribution towards solving increased audience dilemmas. Tactics that have been successful time and time again, include:

- Related reading segments at the end of content to help link topically associated content together and help steer the user through the buying cycle
- Base of page FAQs (frequently asked questions) to clarify jargon and remove information barriers towards conversions
- New data, quotes, opinion and statistics to show that the content is up to date and reflecting any changes since its initial creation
- User-generated content and search terms reflecting latest audience patterns and data changes
- Leverage Google 'suggested search' to see the subtopics that people look for (using the available data), identify gaps in your content and included them with new content you create

Podcasts and webinars. This could include extra content types too; however, the resurgence of voice search means that in increasing number of people want to digest content through audio and other means. For business, this poses an easy to act on growth area, by repurposing existing content into new content types. It's fast and effective, and adds new search vertical wins by getting your content into areas inaccessible previously (limited by content type).

Mobile friendliness. Optimising for mobile enables content to appear for effectively for all devices and reflects the mobile first move from Google initiated in 2018. Making website content responsive by design, increasing mobile (and general) speed, plus organising content that shows awareness of mobile behaviour will progress existing content success.

Reorganise modules. If you think about each website content page as being built up of individual components (or modules), you can look at Google In Page analytics and associated heatmap data to move the most important modules of content into the areas producing the greatest impact. CTA buttons and text, short forms and other event-driven content can all be refined to improve the business value you receive from existing content. Each page of website copy should follow an intended hierarchy or sequence of events, with the most important content first. Examples of this in action can be seen in the content cheat sheets provided in the previous chapter.

Amplification. Identify who the thought leaders and key influencers are on topics your content covers. Create influencer marketing plans to target them, and get them to engage with your content (this can be incentivised too, increasing success rates). This will help you to gain solid external trust signals to help content rank, as well as increase the exposure to the audiences (through the identified influencers) most sought after and impactful for your business.

Visuals. Designing creative content visualisations and building more visual content pieces (consider infographics, listicles, and other content types) regularly get overlooked and dismissed because of the investment of time required. They are, however, incredible ways to get your business in front of new audiences. Adding bespoke pictures to existing content helps with the perceived depth and value of content coverage, increases fresh content signals and supports more effective content skim reading and information digesting. More people share and engage with visual content (helping with social PR and external backlinks), plus the pain point of creating nice imagery, can become a brand differentiator once overcome.

Identifying New Content

Second only to improving your current content is filling gaps in your marketing content. This is your repeatable approach for getting the brand, business, services and products in front of the right people and often as possible.

A content gap is simply an untapped (or unrealised) content topic area, page or type that has not yet been identified and scheduled in as part of your business marketing content.

There are a myriad of ways in which you can approach marketing content gap identification and filling as a business, and now we discuss practical ways to effectively do this, using experience over thousands of successful content campaigns.

Here are the top 10 tactics to find and fill business and marketing content gaps which you can prioritise and act on today.

(1) **Answering audience questions.** As a business, you should be prolific in answering (solving) problems first and providing (at a cost) the solution second. To do this, you need to factor in trend awareness, persona understanding, search behaviour and related topics. All of the data points for this can be free, plus there are paid versions which can expedite the process in some case too. Answer the Public (https://answerthepublic.com/) is a free answer engine, which is perfect for initial topic-based content creation. Other tools including SEMRush, BuzzSumo and aHrefs have paid versions which supply trends around topics and ranking content that normally

includes answering audience pain points. GSC can be filters to show the common who, what, why, where, when, how queries, plus you can interrogate search engines including Google directly for suggested search and relate search result queries. Google Trends, Google Correlate and Twitter Analytics supply free trends data. Google Trends and Correlate to go to for historical timelines and changing trends, Twitter Analytics and other Twitter trend filtering and widgets are perfect for what's happening now and for reactive content gap filling based on current interest. Working with GA, you can generate insights on user behaviour flows, and view patterns on performance, social sharing and other insights for new content building. You can also see all of the on-site searches people used your website search for and compare this to the products, services and content that exist, creating new content for those that are commercially viable but not yet covered within your website copy at present.

(2) **Competitor analysis.** When auditing your own website for content gaps, you need to factor in awareness on top performing and direct competition external websites as well. You can use site search operators in Google (be entering site:any-website-name) and copying/pasting the indexed content into a Google document or Excel file and then comparing/contrasting content gaps on a service, product, category and topic level. This provides meaningful business content gap analysis which can be actioned for known competitor gains. There are tools (for example, SEMRush and aHrefs) where you can add site by site content automated analysis, reducing the manual labour and increasing efficiencies and regularity of competing these type of actions. Competitor analysis for content ideation and fill projects can also include business social media account sharing and posts, content promotion and even to granular levels of who they follow (as part of persona content targeting and building). It is useful to look beyond the brand-level competitor analysis in isolation and incorporate key staff profile follows as well. This will help identify what they (the key people and experts) are speaking about; content they are reading, writing and sharing events they are attending and more. Key staff personal accounts often deliver extended value for content filling as they tend to be less gated and premeditated than the main company business accounts.

(3) **Surveys and forms.** Ask your audience questions and build qualitative data sets created by gathering unique insights. This can be incentivised with free information sharing, free audits and by other means (for example, social media competition entry and prize draw). Keep questions open and targeted to broader application areas. Segment the questions to cater for current audience, potential audience, and influencers for your target audience. Don't overlook the value of previous customers too (they may be more frank than those who you are currently interacting with). As a business, you want to know why motivates your audience, why they initially needed your services/products, how they compared competing alternatives, why they did/did not choose you, and all the pertinent points from first investigation through to final decision. You should also look beyond your audience reach

as well. By including external review sites (for example, Google My Business, TrustPilot and industry-tailored review sites and sources), you can see at the detailed user-generated content and costumer sentiment sharing, then fill these issues and pain points with content that targets them. Reviews are useful ways for generating emotional driven insights, even more so when factoring on competitor reviews.

(4) **Keyword research.** Traditional SEO-led expertise items including keyword research should never go overlooked when ideating missing content and new content opportunities. Free tools like Google Keyword Planner are useful for refining the volume of new and missing opportunities into a body of data that is easy to interrogate, prioritise and act on. From Keyword Planner, you can assess volume and competition to create content gap filling throughout the expected short/medium/longer term impact areas. Outputs from GSC, Answer the Public, GA, Google Trends, etc. can all be inputs into Google Keyword Planner for prioritisation. In the keyword research phase you are often looking for high-potential volume (traffic, impressions) and low-expected competition terms which can be added into the mix within the easy to identify high-competition/high-volume terms usually targeted as hero terms for business. It's important to extend your keyword research phase beyond the standard approaches too. Consider looking at iTunes for podcasts you can create, Amazon for product-based search queries and Wikipedia index topical content for groups of terms and subtopics you are not currently catering for effectively.

(5) **Alerts, notifications and newsletters.** Each industry has key publications, websites and competitors where you can set Google Alerts, Twitter lists, notifications and trends, as well as sign up for newsletters and email updates. The value of this initial effort (it takes 30 minutes to an hour to set up all of this), is the proactive ongoing access to new data. Key terms get mentioned in new indexed Google searches, and you receive alerts. Competitors launch new products and services, and you receive email updates from their newsletters and ad hoc marketing communications. New events, and media content trends in social media, and your Twitter account lists those specific to your followed trends. All of this is easy content fill access driven by changing data and bet of all once you set it up, the insights proactively come to you. You can also use RSS feeds to have content delivered and added to folders in your Outlook account (or other email client) to make it easy to look at new content (including using services like Feedly and the hashtag search feature) to set and receive topics of note.

(6) **Social forums and informational platforms.** Notably Reddit and Quora in this instance, as these are less frequently cited for this purpose and therefore proposed added competitive advantages. Reddit has boundless content fill choices and practical applications. You can sign up for and follow key industry areas and sub Reddits to monitor and find new relevant content entrenching itself with the Reddit community. With Quora (see Chapter 6 for added details), you can watch competitors and thought leaders in action, view the questions and answers people are engaging with, gage interest

levels and content exposure to complete SWOT analysis on your own content auditing looking for gaps. There are sites like Medium which are also growing in opportunity and exposure that you can include in your research.

(7) **Visual social media.** Do not fall into the trap of relying on text-based and informational only social platforms for active and trending new content opportunities. Instagram and Pinterest are useful starting places. Pinterest, for example, has 'collections' that provide a fast overview of data for the most popular posts. You will also want to look at YouTube for video content trends and changes related to your audience plus the industry you operate in. Each of these areas also provides analytical information for you own business accounts to review and include in new content building. You don't want to restrict your new content awareness to limited content types, and the more exhaustive your social listening (and viewing) becomes, the greater the extent of the results you should expect to receive.

(8) **Newsjacking.** As a company, a lot of the new content ideation, research, data and findings can be accessible without incurring most of the idea-tion and resource needs, providing you are ready to act fast. News-jacking is fundamentally repurposing breaking media stories for unique content coverage for you own use and marketing gains. The perquisite for effective newsjacking is fast content curation and implementation so that you are able to maximise the short time frame interest before it diminishes (ideally within the first morning/few hours of a story being released). You can also include content authority building and promo-tion within newsjacking by adding comments, mentions, links and social sharing/PR as tactics to push the content out to interested readers and leveraging the short-term value of the content (even within the content originators' websites, especially when they are mainstream media outlets with vast readership).

(9) **Repeating what works.** Google Analytics is likely to be your primary inward looking tool for this, as you can create content fill areas by leveraging and revisiting prior successes. This can be content types and topics, as well as repeating common characteristics in successful content, plus seasonal wins that can be repeated for new gains. You want to factor in trends at both impression (potential traffic and value) level as well as visits and goal completions/events (actual impact) level. Google Search Console your data source for impressions/potentials, and Google Analytics, for actual impact. Some of the data tips include:

- Set long-term (all-time) timeframes and see repeated peaks on metrics for repeated opportunity
- Review seasonality and compare this with Google Trends for content gaps
- Look at the content performing above average and distil this into topics, pain points, and funnel stages – use this for filling gaps and repeating annual opportunities

- Take the top-performing content areas and compare this to the topics covered externally – listing missing content coverage
(10) **Machine learning, intelligent algorithms and Artificial Intelligence.** Many of the pre-listed options in this top 10 will be leveraging some of the features of these areas to provide data-driven insights; however, in this context, it is about how you can apply these factors to your own data. Chapters 2–4 detail these areas in some detail, so it is a worthwhile exercise to recap them if you are unsure how this can apply for content gap fulfilment or deriving competitive advantages through prescriptive content recommendations. Artificial Intelligence (AI) for content gap filling can help advise your marketing team on items including:

- Factors influencing sales, leads and conversions
- Generating fresh insights and challenging existing assumptions
- Identifying how, where and why people are dropping out of the sales funnels
- Producing content frameworks to create new content
- Collect and distil trends from user data (for example, chatbot conversations)
- Predictive modelling for forecasting content success and opportunities
- Leveraging segmented data sources to understand and fulfil customer experience requirements through content

Your Content Creation Framework

The right content framework can dramatically change your content production method, systematically improving the content worth and its contribution towards your business and marketing goals.

The significance of content building frameworks frequently gets neglected by the focus on content delivery to deadlines and isolated (individual) content performance focus.

Here you get access to a robust and multipurpose content creation framework that can be easily modified for many business requirements.

This framework is intended for you to challenge and improve your current way of developing content and to support a consistent way of making your content better. You need to look at this with an open mind, and some of these areas can need a fresh perspective and objective consideration, and business culture changes or modifications (depending on your current situation).

(1) **Telling the story.** Every piece of content should have four fundamental elements:

- The headline/title – This entices users to click, engage and share. CTR is an important ranking consideration for natural search gains, as are social signals (a correlated signal), backlinks and content/brand mentions. Headline refinements can change mediocre content into top performers and act as click bait tactics to increase content visibility. Tactics including numbers, action words, emotion and other factors can all improve headlines, but ultimately you need to test, refine and improve them with data, as despite repeated trends, each target persona will behave differently.

- The introduction – Reinforces user expectations and drives the user to take action. An effective introduction lowers bounce rates (another ranking factor/correlated signal for high-performing content), increases conversions and sends the user through the buying cycle. Introductions that work, theme the page, promote USPs and get the user to the converting content sooner.

- The main body (middle) – Supports the dominant theme of the page and provides trust signals, expertise and authority. All of which are needed to enable a person to buy and help content rank effectively (you may recall EAT content mentioned earlier in this guide). The middle of the content often excites with mixed content types (images, video, interactive web features) and aids in converting people requiring extra nurturing through the removal of information barriers and other known audience pain points. Users post-scroll require much greater reason to take action and engage, hence the requirement to provide added visual impact and enticement.

- The end (conclusion/summary) – Following traditional storytelling best practices, the ending summarises the key takeaways from the content and reinforces the content purpose and desired user outcome. The end of the content needs to be considered as the final opportunity to give the user every opportunity to make that decision to buy/contact and give you a means to stay in touch. The end of the content can introduce other forms of user value capturing including newsletter/email information retrieval, social sharing and other actions that help contribute towards macro (final) goals and user events.

(2) **Purposely defined workflows.** At this stage of this marketing content guide, it will come as no surprise to you that every piece of content needs to have a clearly defined purpose from the outset. This purpose should have an associated workflow that details each of the necessary steps identified and impacted by the content created to steer the user through the processes towards the final conversion (then into the repeat buyer and brand evangelist process). The awareness and application of content to match the purpose and given workflow marries content with marketing and wider business goals effectively, thus integrating actions with intended outputs and outcomes.

(3) **Briefing process.** Content writers need distinct instruction when it comes to delivering the content output you are looking for. Each new content request (including modifying existing content) needs to have a consistent form of content briefing, plus initial discussion before putting pen to paper. Characteristics of a good content brief comprise:

- Word count
- Persona

- Pitch
- Placement
- Key themes and terms plus framework details (proposed headings)
- Competing best of breed examples
- Delivery date/deadline
- Purpose
- Supporting data/stats/quotes
- Intended outcome (metrics/measurements/performance)
- Contact for queries and contact details
- Source materials

(4) **Review/results/refinement dates.** Content at the point of briefing, must have deadlines set for data analysis in the three areas of review, refine and results. If content works it needs to be analysed, characteristics identified, and frameworks modified to improve, new content gains. Results require sharing, improving internal sentiment or gathering support and budget for key improvements. All content can be viewed as a work in progress; no piece is ever considered completed and new data always provides opportunity for next phases of business wins.

(5) **Differentiation.** This can be driven by a culture of experimentation, data insights and hypothesis testing (consider the data-driven and ecosystem learnings from Chapters 1 and 2 of this guide). The question your content and marketing teams (staff/individuals) need to have as part of their mindset and approach is 'what makes my content special?' Purpose is not enough when lots of competing content examples have the same purpose, but other competitive advantages (budget, expertise, scale, brand power, etc.), reinforce the power of differentiation. This can include saying something new, showcasing new data insights and providing something novel, contradictory to popular belief, or impactful in other ways.

Chapter Summary

The purpose of this section of the business and marketing content guide was to practically deliver processes and approaches for making all of your existing content deliver better results and helping you to find and fill all the priority gaps in your content.

These two areas combined empower marketing teams to become, and remain on top of the content opportunity and make the most out of every word written and image created to increase the returns from you marketing content efforts.

The third part of this chapter focussed on improving and defining a content production method that could systematically improve the value from the content you create and increase its contribution towards your business goals and objectives.

As we move into the penultimate chapter, the focus moves away from data gathering, content ideation and implementation through to evaluating content success. Dedicated attention includes:

- Setting content benchmarks, goals and objectives
- Choosing the right key performance indicators
- Reporting on content results

Definitions

- CMS: Content management system facilitates consistent and effective website (digital content) management. A globally used example of a CMS by many of the largest brands and fortune 500 companies is WordPress. Many forms of CMS exist including off-the-shelf options and bespoke/custom CMS.
- Suggested search (Google): The predicted search queries that Google provides as you type a query into the Google search engine bar. This includes historical data and personalised search functionality when applicable to the search.

Chapter 9

Evaluating Content Success

Ineffective success tracking instigates incorrect content evaluation and under-mines the integrity of marketing content decision-making throughout all levels of business decision-making.

Many content performance control and measurement methods fail to cater for the scope of measurement needed to accurately assess content returns or attribute content metric-based performance back to wider business goals and objectives.

In this chapter, we provide the methods, approaches and practical advice required to report on results; choose the right key performance indicators (KPIs) and set the appropriate benchmarks, goals and objectives (BGOs).

We start with setting the appropriate BGOs.

Setting Benchmarks, Goals and Objectives

I always prefer to have multiple data sources and points of failure when it comes to BGOs.

This is partially down to the fact that no single data point provides the entire data picture, and, secondly, because the layers of information needed to calculate BGO extend beyond the focus of one data or analytics package. I also like to be able to compare and contrast nuances of items including weighting and prioriti-sation of metrics which differ by platform provider.

Setting Benchmarks

There are many possible benchmarks you can use for business and marketing content, and the below will allow you to source your own too. In most cases, the combination of benchmarks you decide on will factor in at least a handful of the below recommendations.

(1) **Internal benchmarks.** Focus is on the internal standard of content perfor-mance compared with similar content items, looking where possible to accurately compare 'like for like'. It is necessary to include year on year (YoY) as well as previous period timeframe comparison to remove season-ality and other industry trends that can skew data. When setting

Data-driven Marketing Content, 133–148
Copyright © 2019 by Emerald Publishing Limited
All rights of reproduction in any form reserved
doi:10.1108/978-1-78973-817-920191010

benchmarks, it is important to adequately account for data outliers and other slanting impact points (for example, paid promotion) so that a fair appraisal can be made. You should incorporate peak, lowest and medium performance measurements as part of your content benchmarking so that you see the full barometer of performance. The main data platforms and analytical tools you will be referencing for this may likely include Google Analytics (GA), Google Search Console (GSC), aHrefs, SEMRush plus other social media data sets and internal data collection including any bespoke data platforms and sales/marketing software (like SalesForce) plus related workflow systems in place. You may also use manual data collection for items like telephone calls and customer sentiment feedback mechanisms.

(2) **External benchmarks.** Outwardly orientated, looking at available external data sets for performance within the wider market, the goal of this is to see how well the content created measures up to everything else available on the same topic/industry/product/expertise area. You should have (if you don't consider setting up) consistent data sources to fairly assess content specific to your industry. This will likely include Google industry benchmark data; YouGov survey results and data; plus other sources of analytical information including Ahrefs top performing content on any given topic, and self-assessment using social media platform specific publicly available data, plus inclusion within aggregate lists, roll-up content and ranking in Google and Bing.

(3) **Data benchmarks.** Underpinning all of the benchmarking approaches, data benchmarks objectify the performance of content and establish agreed levels to which all content should expect to deliver on. Having an expensive set of data benchmarks give businesses the choice to consistently measure progress made and allot budget and resource accordingly.

(4) **Qualitative benchmarks.** An area almost always disregarded by companies when it comes to considering the level of impact and sentiment received from your intended audience. Social signals and data from Twitter and Facebook Analytics (among others), plus sources including BuzzSumo and aHrefs, can supply some of this information, but I always like to include user surveys and other open feedback areas as well. This is also referred to as Sentiment (or audience) benchmarks, but qualitative benchmarking can extend much further than sentiment alone.

(5) **Competition benchmarks.** Using tools like SEMRush, Majestic and Buzz-Sumo, along with manual search engine interrogation for content ranking, you are able to judge how effectively content held up compared to your main competitors. It is useful to include in your competitor benchmarking awareness of information based visibility competition (sites like Wikipedia) that rank for many informational areas, however, are not direct selling threats. The reason for this is that these types of websites are still negatively impacting visibility, traffic (and ultimately sales/conversions) by outranking your content, so should be deemed as barriers to marketing content success.

(6) **General (content type) benchmarks.** There are many content types, and each had distinct merits and flaws that want to be factored into benchmarking by

content type. A video benchmark of metrics would include view time, shares, clicks and social promotion engagement measurements with reach, likes and shares included. A blog post would have alternative measurements for benchmarking comprising visibility, traffic, social shares, new landing page users and visits from Organic Search, and supplemental metrics with internal pageviews. Content type benchmarks enable content to be judged on the appropriate elements it is intended to impact.

(7) **Channel benchmarks.** Organic Search, Paid Advertising, Social Media, emails, and other marketing channels all have definite benchmarks and purposes which mean they need to be considered to impact separate factors. SEO, for example, has the primary role of generating awareness and assisting in sales, goal completions and new business. This means that the benchmark and metric criteria should be skewed towards impressions, clicks, CTR, visits, new users, percentage of total website traffic contribution and assisted conversions, rather than CRO, revenue, transactions and sales/leads orientated gains.

(8) **Best of breed benchmarks.** Factoring internal and external benchmark sets, this is really about aspiring to be the best with your marketing content and always looking to outperform previous peak performance items. As much a mindset as it is a benchmark approach, 'best of breed' demonstrates a numerical understanding of individual content and marketing efforts that have historically delivered the most value. Externally, this will include top ranking and traffic driving competitor content, most shared content articles and those gathering most traction with the audience through backlinks and social sharing.

(9) **Market share benchmarks.** Not the easiest to measure (SEMRush details useful site comparison metrics for this, plus other social, ranking and backlink data can be used as like-for-like performance on identified competitor content and you can also use Google paid/AdWords analytics information for market share contribution), this showcases how much (or little) your content has returned based on the potential that exists within the market your business operates in based on exposure measurements. Market share is an ever-moving benchmark and impacted by many external factors.

Goals and objectives move statements like 'we wanted to improve traffic', 'we need more sales' and 'we need to get more sales from our marketing efforts', into something meaningful and fully measurable.

The prerequisite of goals and objective setting is that they need to be SMART: Specific, Measurable, Attainable, Relevant, and Timely.

Goals give clear instruction on what the marketing and business content sets out to achieve and details the expectations.

Website and content marketing goals can often have department-centric goals (for example, 'deliver 10 new website enquiries', for the sales and marketing teams) as well as holistic success parameters (for example, provide 10,000 impressions, 750 visits, 500 social shares), which can then be set per marketing channel (SEO, PPC, Direct, Referral and Email are the frequently cited ones).

Many of the largest global organisations (including Google) rely on creating and cultivating a culture of objectives (and key results) to maximise all levels within their business to aligned and integrated goals.

As a practical example of Objectives and Key Results (OKRs) in action, companies I have worked with have used OKR systems to do the following:

- Expedite goal achievement
- Integrate all staff towards collective goals
- Gamify and incentivise individuals and teams
- Share company targets and ambitions
- Motivate teams
- Increase consistency of effort toward key result areas
- Communicate progress
- Introduce new concepts
- Improve consistency and benchmarks for knowledge, training and development

Examples of OKRs can include the following. The timeframe for these are quarterly, but you can set monthly and other frequency OKRs suitable to your business goals.

Objective:
Increase department revenue by 30%.

Key Results:

(1) Improve the response times to sales requests from 2 days to 1 day
(2) Create new sales proposal documents to increase point of sale value (2 documents)
(3) Attend 10 sales meetings to help with expertise delivery pre-sale

Objective:
Improve customer happy sentiment by 50%.

Key Results:

(1) Survey all customers at start and end of the quarter for sentiment (happy) benchmark and results (500)
(2) Ensure every (100%) customer receives weekly communication
(3) Update company marketing and communications (email and newsletter) to include case studies and user-generated content

Tips for OKR Setting:

- Include the individuals in the ideation process to help with buy-in
- Incentivise OKRs to increase contribution and staff motivation
- Make it easy for staff to log progress for easy achievement success

- Gamify OKRs to make them more engaging and reflective of improvement made
- Ensure OKRs are actively discussed in team and company meetings to reinforce importance
- Use external software to take advantage of tried and tested frameworks
- Ensure all OKRs are stretch-goal based – 60% to 70% completion should be the end goal

Moving onto goal and objectives types that are applicable for website marketing content objectives, a few of those I have experienced having most use for businesses include those detailed next.

- **Drive brand awareness.** Measured by brand search queries, traffic and users to brand pages on your website and social media exposure. A SMART goal would be 'Increase the volume of search queries that include our brand name by 20%, through the delivery of four blog posts and eight social shares, including paid promotion between December 2019 and January 2020. 1,500 visits and 900 new users are required from Organic Search as landing pages entries by 31 January 2020 to new blog pages on the website'.
- **Improve blog performance.** Measurements would typically include volume of ranking terms for the bog, YoY performance of blog pages spanning key metrics, engagement signals (social shares, video watching), pages viewed, time on site, internal pageviews, etc. The SMART goal for this could be 'We intend to increase the landing page traffic to our blog by 10,000 unique visitors per month (2,500 unique visitors per week). We will achieve this by increasing the blogs created from 10 to 20 per month and refreshing the existing top-performing blog posts for another phase of business and marketing content gains'.
- **Increase market share.** This goal/objective requires added specificity as it can be difficult to measure otherwise and you need to remove assumption and subjectivity also. Market share could be based on location, personas, individual competition and span many metric areas (impressions, social sharing, traffic, new users, etc.) A SMART goal would be 'Grow UK website traffic market share by 20% in Q2 2020 for commercial landing pages spanning SEO, PPC, Direct and Referral traffic sources'.
- **Nurture leads.** Acquisition measurements focus on CRO, enquiry and sales numbers, plus micro events tracked through the sales process. Often detailed within drip feed marketing campaigns, the end goal is to get people through the sales cycle faster and generating increased ROI from content and marketing efforts/investments. Lead nurturing approaches require tailoring to reflect the stages within the buying cycle the person is in, and as such the persona can also be specified if it helps to clarify this. A standard SMART goal example for lead nurturing being 'Increase total website events tracked in GA over the next quarter by 40% to support revenue gains of 15% over the same timeframe compared to last year. This will be achieved through

targeted underperformance pages updates and performance boosting using YoY on traffic and revenue data in GA, plus the addition of five new content landing pages created based on competitor product gap analysis already completed'.

- **Increase Organic Search traffic.** Taking note of the channel (in this case Organic Search, impacted by SEO), the most common business goals tend to focus on channels and marketing mediums which they believe can contribute more towards total website and business objective areas. An associated SMART goal for this could be 'By 30 September 2020, I want to increase our Organic Search traffic by 20%. This will be achieved by focussing on optimising and boosting the value derived from our top 10 traffic landing pages as well as the high impression/low click (CTR top 20 opportunity pages) and building five new hero content pieces based on our audience profiling pain points discussed in our last marketing meeting. Content promotion activities will encourage fresh social signals, PR and authority value to these pages, helping them rank higher and increase CTR'.
- **Improve customer sentiment.** Sentiment is a useful objective area for business as it humanises targets and supplements the value you will expect to gain from improvements in other areas (traffic, new users and more). When setting SMART goals tied to sentiment, you need to prioritise the method for data collection and consider the timeframes for impact. A useful SMART goal for customer sentiment which supports performance wins in other areas is reviews. An example would be 'Increase 5 star rated Google My Business (GMB) reviews from 150 to 400 by the end of the current financial year. This is achieved by incentivising front-line staff to prompt for positive customer review feedback (with retail outlet vouchers) and include GMB review requests in content form completions and post-sale thank you pages'.

If it helps, you can also segment SMART goals into the component parts and reverse engineer the end goal as in the next examples.

Increase Podcast Downloads Goal Example

Specific:
I want to increase the number of downloads for the podcasts in out podcast section of the website by improving the optimisation of the section; expanding the content depth and coverage (including podcast transcript creation) and promoting podcasts through social media, email and associated business marketing channels.

Measurable:
Compared to last year, we want to see a 50% increase in landing page (all sources) website traffic to all URLs that include 'podcast', and a 20% increase in podcast downloads, both measured in GA.

Attainable:
The previous targeted podcast project saw an increase in landing page traffic to the podcast section of 15% and 10% increase in direct podcast downloads, without the inclusion of paid marketing and limited Organic Search optimisation.

Relevant:

Podcasts educate and inform our audience. They extend our marketing reach and target identified audience persona areas. When our podcasts increase traffic and download volumes, they also directly contribute towards leads and sales.

Timely:

Outcomes are expected by 15 May 2020.

SMART Goal:

By 15 May 2020, we will see a 50% increase in landing page (all sources) website traffic to all URLs that include 'podcast' and a 20% increase in podcast downloads. This will be achieved through podcast website improvements including the optimisation of the section, expanding the content depth and coverage (including podcast transcript creation) and promoting podcasts through social media, email, and associated business marketing channels.

Choosing the Best KPIs

The best KPIs are those most reflective of your business goals and objectives, and suitable for easy facilitation and assessment of content performance.

They (KPIs) should automatically accommodate for most of the business and marketing reporting needs (removing reporting overlap and resource waste), and cater for all important layers of stakeholder and staff informational needs.

KPIs can be department specific but should include integrated and cross-department measurements as well.

By setting and tracking the right KPIs, a company can make more informed and smarter business content and marketing decisions by factoring in the success levels of current and historical projects.

KPIs are the measurement aspect of BGO, standardising success assessment and fuelling company reporting.

KPIs can cover a myriad of metric areas, many were included in the previous section where we discussed setting company BGOs and SMART goals.

Selecting the right (best) KPIs can seem overwhelming for many small- and medium-sized businesses; however, in the KPI lists provided, this should become a much simpler activity.

Before we delve into the granularity of the KPI lists, the main types of KPIs for marketing and business content comprise e-Commerce, topic, sales, marketing, channel, medium, content type, online, off-line, integrated, social, internal, external and others.

It may be a worthwhile exercise to refamiliarize yourself with the objective setting types discussed earlier in this chapter if you are unsure about the KPI types, as these directly correlated with the goal and objective areas.

Key Performance Indicator Lists

It is almost impossible to list a completely exhaustive list of business marketing content KPIs; however, those most pertinent to this practical guide are detailed next.

Common Content Marketing and Business Content Metrics

There are numerous repeated inclusion measurements (metrics) for viewing the success of business marketing content campaigns, and these tend to include:

(1) Impressions and exposure
(2) Social shares and engagement
(3) Traffic (sessions/visits): new and repeat
(4) Users: new and return
(5) CTR
(6) Average rank (position tied to pages/topic/terms)
(7) Backlinks and mention (related to topic and URLs)
(8) Email and newsletter opt-ins (micro goal completions)
(9) GA events (specific to the pages/campaign)

Revenue Metrics

Revenue-targeted content for marketing campaign metrics would normally cover the below (note: although some of these are traditionally paid advertising items (for example, CPC and CPA), they can also be easily calculated form time/resource and investment to any other marketing channel):

(1) Conversion rate
(2) CPC (cost per click)
(3) CPA (cost per acquisition)
(4) ROI
(5) Traffic and new users
(6) Events and goal completions
(7) Assisted conversions

You may also look to factor into these internal measurements inclusive of:

(1) Lead to close/conversion rate
(2) Quote to close/conversion rate
(3) Lead quality (qualitative metric on a scale of 1–10)
(4) Sales close time (in days)
(5) Average sale value

Channel-Targeted Metrics

As you would anticipate, the measurement for an email marketing campaign accomplishments would differ dramatically from that of a paid advertising campaign on Facebook.

For example, metrics for email marketing content measuring would typically cover:

(1) Open rate %
(2) Event clicks

(3) Replies (total)
(4) Forwards
(5) Opt-ins

You could also factor in negative sentiment metrics as well, for example:

(1) Unsubscribe requests

A social media measurement plan would cover the below and related metrics:

(1) Shares
(2) Likes
(3) Follows
(4) Mentions
(5) Engagement (total)
(6) Replies (direct messages (DM))
(7) Comments
(8) Website social media:

- Traffic
- Events and goal completions
- Assisted conversions

Link and Authority-Building Metrics

Backlinks and mentions from content are two of the primary authority building areas for any business looking to grow Organic Search results from the main search engines (notably Google and Bing, but others as well, including Baidu, as the main search engine in China) and increase referral traffic coming to websites and other online entities.

Metrics to judge successful link and authority content campaigns specific to the content/topic/URLs include:

(1) New backlinks and mentions (total)
(2) Referral traffic
(3) Social media:

- Shares
- Likes
- Follows
- Mentions
- Engagement (total)
- Replies (direct messages (DM))
- Comments

(4) External backlinks and mention quality and value signals:

- Domain rating (DR) and authority (DA)
- Followed links (authority passing)

- Unique linking domains
- Domain location
- Domain relevancy (qualitative score 1–10)
- Source and medium
- C-class IPs
- Anchor text
- Trust and citation flow

Google Analytics Dimensions and Metrics

As GA will be the primary source for many of the metrics your business will be referring to, here are the GA-dominant dimensions and metrics available to you, relevant for your content performance measurements (this same approach can be used for Google Search content for pre-click metrics areas including impressions, clicks, CTR and more).

To clarify, a dimension can be seen as the 'what' information telling you the details and attributes of website visitors, whilst metrics detail how the dimension is measured providing numerical data (numbers/values).

As an example of this in practice, the dimension 'user type' would tell you what type of user (for example, new or returning) landed on your website in Google Organic Search, the metrics would tell you how many users (total, new, returning) landed on the site, how long they spent on the website, how many pages they viewed and more.

Next are segmented lists of GA metrics available to you at the time of writing. These do not cover all of the GA metrics available but summarise many of the most useful ones for the purposes of this section of the guide.

GA user metric examples:

(1) % New Sessions
(2) 1 Day Active Users
(3) 14 Day Active Users
(4) 28 Day Active Users
(5) 30 Day Active Users
(6) 7 Day Active Users
(7) New Users
(8) Number of Sessions per User
(9) Users

GA session metric examples:

(1) Average Session Duration
(2) Bounce Rate
(3) Bounces
(4) Hits
(5) Session Duration
(6) Sessions

GA Lifetime value (and cohort) tracking metric examples:

(1) Appviews per User
(2) Appviews per User (LTV)
(3) Goal Completions per User
(4) Goal Completions per User (LTV)
(5) Pageviews per User
(6) Pageviews per User (LTV)
(7) Revenue per User
(8) Revenue per User (LTV)
(9) Session Duration per User
(10) Session Duration per User (LTV)
(11) Sessions per User
(12) Sessions per User (LTV)
(13) Total Users
(14) User Retention
(15) Users

GA AdWords (Google Ads) metric examples:

(1) Clicks
(2) Cost
(3) Cost per Conversion
(4) Cost per Goal Conversion
(5) Cost per Transaction
(6) CPC
(7) CPM
(8) CTR
(9) Impressions
(10) ROAS (Return on advertising spend)

GA goal conversion metric examples:

(1) Abandoned Funnels
(2) Goal Completions
(3) Goal Conversion Rate
(4) Goal Starts
(5) Goal Value
(6) Goal 'Value' Abandoned Funnels
(7) Goal 'Value' Abandonment Rate
(8) Goal 'Value' Completions
(9) Goal 'Value' Conversion Rate
(10) Goal 'Value' Value
(11) Per Session Goal Value
(12) Total Abandonment Rate

GA page tracking metric examples:

(1) % Exit
(2) Average Time on Page
(3) Entrances
(4) Entrances/Pageviews
(5) Exits
(6) Page Value
(7) Pages/Session
(8) Pageviews
(9) Time on Page
(10) Unique Pageviews

GA event tracking metric examples:

(1) Average Value
(2) Event Value
(3) Events/Session with Event
(4) Sessions with Event
(5) Total Events
(6) Unique Events

GA e-commerce tracking metric examples:

(1) Average Order Value
(2) Average Price
(3) Average QTY
(4) Ecommerce Conversion Rate
(5) Per Session Value
(6) Product Adds To Cart
(7) Product Checkouts
(8) Product Detail Views
(9) Product List Clicks
(10) Product List CTR
(11) Product List Views
(12) Product Refund Amount
(13) Product Refunds
(14) Product Removes From Cart
(15) Product Revenue
(16) Product Revenue per Purchase
(17) Quantity
(18) Quantity Added To Cart
(19) Quantity Checked Out
(20) Quantity Refunded
(21) Quantity Removed From Cart

(22) Revenue
(23) Revenue per User
(24) Transactions
(25) Transactions per User
(26) Unique Purchases

Reporting on Results

Building on the company goals and objective areas and metrics (measurements) for attributing amounts and values to expectations, reporting is the visualisation element of evaluating content success.

Effective business reporting supports easy content performance and progress analysis, whilst facilitating content marketing discussion and decision-making (including investment choices).

The main considerations for marketing content reports are detailed now.

- **Steering insights.** Metrics can be used in all sorts of ways, and the same data sets can provide completely different reporting insights depending on the application by the report creator and data analyst. For integrity reasons, report focus should be consistent and related to the repeated set of business goals and objectives. Summary sections can effectively conclude the extra insights and overview information, but report coverage should not be skewed to overlook unwanted attention of areas in decline or requiring improvement.
- **Telling a story.** Storytelling through reporting places data and insights into context and assists report readers with seeing progress made towards goals and objectives, with reinforcement of what still needs to be accomplished. Reporting without guidance on the bigger picture reduces the scope and value derived.
- **Interactivity.** There are many tools which enable interactive reporting including GA custom reports and dashboard, plus Microsoft PowerBI. Interactive reports can be built from templates, shared with varying permission levels and provide real-time insights for fast-paced industries and department requirements. Data visualisation is fast becoming a reporting norm for larger organisations and needs to be considered for small to medium sized businesses (SMBs) as well. By providing interactive data, you open the report to additional data interrogation and tailored cross team use, all within the same controlled reporting template. Reports should not be seen as isolated insight documents but ongoing refined and long-term trend platforms that can provide ongoing use and value to business regardless of size and data sets.
- **Integrated.** Having worked both in-house and agency side of content creation and marketing for many years, I've had first-hand experience of receiving and delivering huge amounts of bespoke and templated reports, and without any hesitation, the most frustrating aspect of them are segmented and individualised reports for every service being delivered. The frustrations include:
  - Report inconsistencies and overlap
  - Retainer time inefficiencies/internal resource waste

- Contrasting data and insights
- Conflicting focus areas
- Data oversights and limitations from fragmented data sets
- Excessive reading, reviewing and self analysis
- **Core metric sets.** Briefly mentioned previously, there is a requirement to identify, agree, set, and maintain a consistent base layer of metrics, closely matched and relevant to the fundamental business goals. Whilst marketing campaigns will vary, the fundamentals rarely change when it comes down to the primary business goals and performance KPIs. Never omit metrics because they underwhelm or provide negative performance signals. A report should not be a selection of gains and highlights, it should be an accurate, balanced assessment of where you are related to primary business objectives.
- **Templated.** Reports should not be custom built or amended every time they are created. Data need refreshing, new highlights and summary content revised, but other than that, a majority of the report should remain the same with only the data sets being updated (in most cases automatically updated). The reports provided should be refined for bespoke customer (internal and external customer) provision and situational understanding, and the repeat value provision led by communicating data change, progress context (through effective storytelling) and reinforcement of what has been completed to impact the data, plus the proposed next focus actions to support new goal progress.
- **The business case.** Reports are completely redundant without placing the data into the context of the business needs. Citing CTR, CPA, CPC, reach, visibility, bounce rates, and other information without an appropriate business logic is simply baffling report recipients, not informing, including, steering or cultivating business relationships. Always keep in mind that reports are intended for the recipients' benefit primarily, not just a tool to dictate narrow viewpoints for the people/companies delivering and presenting them.
- **Communication tools.** Effective reports stem conversation, discussion and debate. When running through a report with a customer or internal stakeholder, it is necessary to pause intermittently, verify that your assumptions and findings are consistent with the outcomes everyone else is deriving and clarify any queries and misunderstanding. Reports should not be something completed and sent by email without follow-up discussion. When creating reports, you should ask yourself 'What new insights am I providing?', 'What are the main takeaways?' and 'What is the purpose of this slide/segment/section of the report?' This will help keep a value focus for reports and limit the stagnation of them over the short to medium term.
- **Review and refinement.** There need to be schedule review and refinement timeframes for your reports. This helps you to push back on constant tweaking by setting expectations and putting in place feedback loops, plus it gives the people delivering and receiving the reports the opportunity to contribute towards improving them.
- **Seasonal consideration.** YoY, as well as previous period data interrogation and provision, helps overcome seasonal trends and data skewing. While you may

opt to focus on YoY trends, you want to be able to demonstrate short-term impact too (for example, the impact on CTR with advert updates). The association between actions completed and impact made are crucial if you want your reports to be the main reference point for assessing progress and performance gains.

- **Managing up, down and sideways.** You may wish to vary the report pitch, tone and story reflective of the audience you are sharing it with. When managing up, added focus on brevity matters, as time allocation and key staff availability reduces with senior staff (often attention spans decline too). When reporting to your peers, focus is likely to cater for increased audience participation and debate. By contrast, when managing down to less experienced members of your team or company, the storytelling element of reports are likely to become more prescriptive and guidance based with limited justification and discussion.
- **Customer centric.** The customer in the case of reporting is the person/people who are the intended audience receiving the report. Each element of the report (text, image, chart and interactive feature) should be created with the customer in mind. The reports are not meant to please you or fulfil your needs, they are intended to place the customer at the centre of the report, catering for their preferences and information/insight inclinations.
- **Intuitive.** Charts, tables, interactive features and slides all need to be easy to digest and intuitive for the user. Very little narrative should be required with the use of the right imagery and data visuals. If you show your report slides/segments to a handful of different people with varying degrees of data familiarity, they should all come to close assumptions of what the data are telling them. If they don't, the report is not as clear as it needs to be.
- **Frequency.** Reports should have delivery dates agreed and adhered to. People will rely on timeliness of report delivery so that they can repeatedly factor in the report value into their regular working activities. For example, people may be using insights from your report for repurposing in their own marketing meetings and key stakeholder meetings. Failing to be timely with reports will lead to reduced use and perceived value.
- **Naming conventions.** The first thing a person sees before they open a report is generally the file name, title or website address of the report. The same as an advert title sets the scene in paid and Organic Search advertising, the naming convention of titles/file names sets the tone for reports. Countless times I've had reports provided with incorrect file names, spelling mistakes and unwanted template characteristics in place (including the wrong customer name!). This removes all validity and integrity of the report and applies a negative sentiment filter to everything else contained within the report.
- **Positive and proactive.** These are two fundamental parts of report positioning. Reports are your opportunity to showcase the efforts applied, the impact made and the opportunity that still exists. If your reports are neutral in sentiment, and reactive by nature (always looking backwards), the feeling they convey is one of stagnation and limited foresight. You need to balance this by including some level of forward thinking, projection-based (forecasting) information (ideally driven by data, machine learning models, or even basic statistical

projections) injecting proactivity and action into your updates. Reports are fantastic means to show that you care, explain why the course of action taken matters and gather buy-in by demonstrating your credulity and expertise.
- **Sequential.** The reports you provide should follow and anticipate logical process and structure. Each slide in a presentation, or page in a document, should naturally lead on from the previous point made and continue the storytelling aspect towards an expected and logical end point. You can include 'wow' moments and stand out stats to re-establish attention and break up complicated data sets, but use this approach sparingly as not to undermine the credibility of the information supplied.

In addition to the previous characteristics of successful business and marketing content report approaches, pay attention to detail, increase the readability of your reports and expedite access to insights as much as possible – people want to be able to skim through reports efficiently without missing pertinent points.

Chapter Summary

The entire focus of this chapter was to empower your business to accurately and effectively evaluate the success of the business and marketing content you create.

Detailed attention was paid towards setting the right BGOs, choosing the best KPIs and aligning them to your goals, with this leading into in data visualisation and better reporting on results.

New concepts introduced included OKRs and SMART goals, plus key characteristics of successful reports were discussed in some detail.

The final chapter of this complete data-driven content guide for business culminates in the future of data-driven content, specifically:

- The role of the machine
- The role of the human
- Human/computer collaboration

Definitions

- Managing up: the process of effectively showing your credibility and expertise to your direct managers and senior staff.
- Managing down: effectively communicating to direct staff you manage and those within less senior roles in the organisation you work for. Through experience levels, job titles and assumed pay scales, you can also manage up, down and sideways within external environments.
- Managing sideways: peer communication with employees working at the same (and similar) job roles, responsibilities and pay scales as yourself.

Chapter 10

The Future of Data-driven Content

It was only a generation ago that the Internet was introduced to and adopted by the mass market, and look at the impact this has had in every area of life, including marketing content and writing generally.

We are living in a data-driven age, one where we have information pushed onto us everywhere we look, and those actively seeking to gather big data find themselves having access to too much too soon, restricting the end results and insights achieved.

Marketers are experiencing new data pain points and are all too frequently becoming overwhelmed with too much information to process, or make meaning from, and we are only at the start of this data-led marketing and business journey.

Once we incorporate Artificial Intelligence (AI), Machine Learning (ML), and the supporting roles of technologies such as intelligent algorithms, Virtual Reality (VR), Augmented Reality (AR), screenless search, voice search, and changing technologically fuelled behaviour (consider the growth of home assistants like Amazon Alexa), it can be daunting playing field for marketing teams and content creators, but that doesn't have to be the case.

The physical characteristics of emotional triggers including fear and anxiety are the same as those experienced through anticipation and excitement, the skewing element is the psychological association to any given event.

Many content writers, creative content developers and marketing experts (including offline, digital and associated areas) cannot wait for these data revolution to settle down; however, this is simply not going to happen in the foreseeable future.

There is, however, still time to embrace this sweeping change and derive a competitive business advantage whilst the mainstream companies are attempting to figure things out.

In this final chapter of the data-driven marketing content guide, we share the latest roles that machines are having within the realm of content production, the role that humans need to play, plus the collaboration between humans and computers.

Data-driven Marketing Content, 149–164
Copyright © 2019 by Emerald Publishing Limited
All rights of reproduction in any form reserved
doi:10.1108/978-1-78973-817-920191011

The Role of the Machine

Computers, robots and machines have more marketing content capabilities today than at any other stage of existence. The main technology improvements that now facilitate complete artificial content creation include the following:

Artificial Intelligence (AI): also referred to as computer and machine intelligence. This is the increasing capabilities for machines to demonstrate intelligence traditionally attributed to human learning (and other animals).

Machine Learning (ML): a brand of AI, this (ML) relates to computers that have the ability to learn based on data sets (partial and complete) by deriving new meaning and insights from data. ML is the study of algorithms and mathematical models used by computers to raise the performance for identified sets of tasks.

Intelligent Algorithms: driven by the creation and application of sets of rules and processes to follow, intelligent algorithms provide effective and consistent approaches to removing typically repeated human tasks. Any process-led or decision tree set of actions completed with a computer can be replicated through the use of intelligent algorithms.

Natural Language Processing (NLP): computer programs that have the ability to analyse and synthesise speech and text processing. A subfield of Computer Science and Artificial Intelligence, NLP has a core focus of the interactions and communications between humans and machines.

Natural Language Generation (NLG): another subfield of Computer Science and Artificial Intelligence, NLG is a program that turns data into language (often creating new text and content).

Chatbots: computer programs that can also be AI, that facilitate and lead human/computer communication often supported by decision tree functionality and predetermined desired conversational outcomes. In most cases, chatbots are text or audio input fuelled. Chatbots are deployed by businesses to simulate natural conversation (and conversational commerce) on a 24/7 basis.

Virtual Assistants (VAs): computer software that provides professional, technical, administrative and informational assistance in domestic and/or commercial settings. At the time of writing this guide, Amazon Alexa is the market leading Virtual Assistant in the home (domestic) market. VAs work with action sets that enable them to go beyond information provision and into taking action from voice triggers. This can include turning lights on/off, reading stories, telling jokes, providing directions and more.

There are many real-world applications of machines for business outside of the content remit we focus on next, including:

- Fraud detection
- Customer services and support
- Online security
- Driverless cars

The Role of Machines in Marketing Content

Regardless of how 'machine ready' your business is at the moment, an important strategy to incorporate into your company content and marketing approaches include awareness, understanding and experimenting with AI plus its related fields and subsets.

Practical factors to consider include asking yourself how your company can increase efficiencies with the use of intelligent algorithms and where machine learning and AI can be included within your current processes to achieve greater results.

Elements of AI are already prolific in the ideation, creation, analysis and reporting on business/marketing content, and it's a safe bet to project this growth to continue at a substantial rate moving forward.

The Internet is abundant with predictions on 'machines taking over the world' and 'machines replacing jobs'; however, the opportunity at present is based on leveraging the isolation and integrated working of machines and humans to make the best out of both.

The primary opportunities from machines for marketing content are listed now. These are accessible to business now.

(1) **Descriptive and predictive analysis.** Telling you what has happened and detailing why, plus forecasting and estimating future change, opportunity and threats based on statistical analysis and other mathematical and machine learning/AI modelling. Advantages of this include efficient drip feeding of insights and increased data change awareness for content and marketing teams to act on. For content writing, this could be something as simple as predicting content topics to write using seasonal trend data of top-performing historical marketing content or providing data narrative for reports. To see this in a real-world setting, you can look at applications including Narrative Science (Quill).

(2) **Data visualisation and interactive reporting.** Providing multiple layers of reporting insights by migrating away from static report functionality. Computer applications and software packages facilitate constant data refresh and real-time reporting functionality for companies. Gains from this include increased reporting value and reduced manual labour required for repeat reporting. Related to marketing content, this would include increasing the impact of content marketing success towards business goals and objectives for justifying increased budget allocation. An example of this in action is Heliograf developed by *The Washington Post* to produce short reports.

(3) **Prescriptive data opportunities and advice.** Including SWOT analysis prescribed actions and potential action prioritisation. This (prescriptive opportunities and advice flagging) involves computers using predetermined (and in some cases this can open up to self-taught) decision tree application of processes and approach towards data changes and new data sets, for proactively advising people on suggested next actions and focus areas. The

business wins here are consistent application and action awareness on data changes, plus the proactivity of identifying and sharing content and marketing opportunities as they arise. A practical example of this could include advising your marketing team of new trending new articles and socially trending topics which competitors are being included within, but your company is not.

(4) **Integrated insights.** By recombining disparate and diverse data sets, machines are able to generate new levels of combined and integrated insights. Whilst humans can look to follow some of the processes to manually replicate this, the time required for data gathering, refinement, processing and associated areas removes the business feasibility for doing so and certainly never delivers anywhere near the scale or frequency that machines can complete this. For a company marketing advantage, this includes unique expertise application and taking action on content opportunities first.

(5) **Seamless content workflows.** AI will enable a more intuitive and repeatable workflow that begins with data-driven content ideation and progresses through content writing and promotion to influencers and persona targets, right through to expediting content access through chatbots and drip feed marketing related to people's latest interaction. For business and marketing content, this helps increase the consistency of performance and places the content marketers' expertise higher up within the content delivery (at the content refinement stages of making the content process more effective as well as improving approaches, frameworks and end results).

(6) **Gap fulfilment.** Data-orientated content discovery supports known actions (like finding content gaps and missing content subtopics) enabling your business to provide increased content depth and completeness of coverage by knowing all of the related and relevant potential opportunities and supplementing this with the metrics required to make fast content decisions. Machines can deliver all of this information at a frequency and data-led prioritisation that empowers teams to react to the opportunity as it happens.

(7) **Content writing.** Automated AI, reports, blogs, articles and journalism are already present and growing in regard to market adoption and use. Any forms of content that follow a detailed structure and approach but differ based on data, trends and statistics, arguably should be created by machines. The benefits of this for companies include faster, consistent and reliable content creation that is free from spelling and grammar mistakes. The guaranteed and timely delivery support sentiment gains plus the quality of outcome are independent of time of day, stress levels, day of the week, or workload (that you would commonly associate with humans). One of the most widely cited NLP examples of machines writing content direct to users is The Associated Press (Wordsmith by Automated Insights).

(8) **Increased volume.** As with all forms of automation, a typical expected (and in most cases realised) outcome is efficiency of delivery and increased

outputs. The automation of business marketing content (even automating elements of content, frameworks and first drafts) will dramatically improve the volume of content created and human resource requirement. The common trait of machine inclusion within content for business is that the human requirement becomes increasingly specialised and the mundane and bulk of the content heavy lifting becomes machine driven and automated. The same is true in this example.

(9) **Handling complexity.** The average person has many more (often 10+) marketing touchpoints before they commit to purchase. This is twice the touchpoints typically seen less than five years ago. The growth in mobile, voice search, wearable technology and ease of which people can gather fast data insights for transactional comparison has all added to this marketing complexity. Computer analytics packages and deep data platforms take away most of the increased data burden and complexity, giving marketers and companies the insights as opposed to all of the data mining and interrogation.

(10) **Content promotion.** Targeting the best prospects, building influencer marketing lists and pushing content out to external websites are all better serviced within machine data frameworks. Machines can explore data sets with trigger words, trends data based on topical themes, following decision tree processes to provide suggested content promotion plans. Machines can then follow these approved plans through predetermined workflows towards complete content promotion campaigns. Using historical data, machines can quickly process best of breed, and top competing ranking content backlinks for prescribed target sites, detailing which should be approached first, and organising actions tied to quality measurements and other traditional humanistic intelligence judgements.

(11) **Company growth.** The role of machines in marketing content are fast becoming one of many wider roles that machines are taking on. This involves increased strategic inclusion in company investment, diversification and growth. The reduced reliance on people numbers (through machines taking on the mundane and volume actions, combined with people migrating to fewer role positions, and higher specialism areas) means that companies can compete more successfully with larger brands reducing some of the impact of scales of economy. This broader company role of machines is closely matched with the increased expectations of machines becoming more prolific in many company areas.

(12) **'Story-making'.** In this guide, we've discussed the need for storytelling many times, but story-making is something empowered directly by machines in content creation. Every data set includes unique data-led story-making potential. You can even build machine learning models with the entire purpose of telling you something new from you data, and using clustering approaches to identify trends, opportunities, audience sentiment and more.

(13) **Deeper insights.** Whether it is needle in the haystack untapped content opportunities or making more out of the untapped data for creating audience reflective marketing content, AI, machine learning, and intelligent

algorithms will increase the depth and volume of insights identified and acted upon to generate business results.

(14) **Interactive content.** There is nothing new about interactive content, but it still fails to appear anywhere near as often as it could be for SMBs. Using computer programs, you are able to repurpose existing content and leverage its social sharing, PR, and engagement metrics with more exciting content type creation. It is unlikely that in the short term, interactive content will replace the more traditional text and image-based content seen in blogs, news and other website mediums; they are already revitalising marketing results and breathing fresh life (and results based value) into business marketing content.

(15) **Performance gains.** Added machine involvement throughout the content process increases the likelihood of content performing closer to its optimum. Whether the content purpose is lead generation, brand exposure or audience education and information purposes, machines can facilitate better results based on historical performance, external data sources and top-performing content characterisation.

(16) **Resurfacing content.** A dominant content production failure is overlooking the repeat potential for content to resurface for new phases of business gains long after its initial inception. With machines providing social listening, trend monitoring and media awareness into your marketing alerts and updates processes, you can resurface and repurpose historical content with limited effort and optimum gains.

(17) **Increased engagement.** Leading us back to increased metric gains from ML and intelligent algorithm insights, increasing content engagement with data-led CTAs, heatmap data source use and on page/in-content refinements, you can maximise the engagement effectiveness of content. This supports perceived content value, impacting content results in areas such as SEO.

The Role of the Human

Unlike many expert assessments and mainstream media focus when it comes down to the future role of people in business and marketing content, I have a much more optimistic outlook and will explain why.

Most technological advancements are built for the purposes of making things easier, faster and more consistent. And while the progression of computers and AI specifically now incorporate levels of creativity plus other supplemental qualities, at a fundamental level, the main focus of these developments still pertain to the 'easier, faster and more consistent' methodology.

The role that people bring to the fore outside of data-driven intelligence include emotional motivations, personal bias, and qualitative subjective experience which, when effectively supported by data, can produce something unique and special.

Regardless of how successful data collection and processing can be, and despite all of the isolated data-led successes that machines repeatedly produce, replicating outputs more reliably than any human being ever could compete with, there are the eureka moments that people provide that cannot be captured, distilled, replicated or processed. In the main, this inability to replicate 'wow' moments is based on the fact that we do not understand them completely ourselves.

The following points reinforce the role of the human in marketing content, we move onto human/computer collaboration last.

(1) **Emotional awareness.** Content can make people laugh, cry, shout, scream and instigate all manners of reactions based primarily on emotional triggers. The global success of the John Lewis Christmas advertisements is a perfect example of this. Prior to a single airing on television, people are excited about what the next advertising campaign will be. There is little doubt that data and machines will have had some degree of inclusion in the marketing content ideation process; however, ultimately the purpose of these TV Christmas adverts is emotional association. Even through qualitative data sourcing, perfecting emotion to the degree required for genuine human association and reaction is something humans are best place to deliver.

(2) **The art of storytelling.** Data can tell a story, but there is an art of storytelling which is undisputedly human. The ability for people to paint a picture through words, call upon memories to contextualise and humanise content and install nostalgic sentiment from audience familiarity and self-association is a truly human quality. The application of memories and anecdotes within marketing content have the power to lift the impact of outputs to create something memorable, shareable and able to support brand evangelism.

(3) **Tone of voice.** Tone of voice comes from people not companies, and not computers. One of the reasons that blogs can have such an impact on traffic and brand visibility is that the content tone comes from the people writing the blogs. Frequently the most followed blogs are those that have numerous content writers, all with the freedom to express tone and personality through their blog posts.

(4) **Language evolution.** Language itself is a malleable tool which humans misuse, modify and change at will, sometimes leading to brand new language phraseology and nuances, at other times short-term, limited span (forgettable) content crazes (think about the 1990s and the inclusion of 'cowabunga' in the English Oxford Dictionary). It is difficult to place any logical certainty towards why terms like cowabunga ever existed, but they transform people through content into sentimental times gone by – a key tool in the human marketers' content toolkit.

(5) **Relatability.** Humans cannot relate to computers, it is not feasible. A vast majority of marketing and business content include tonality and pitch supporting relatability of the subject matter and the expertise of the writers to the identified audience personas being targeted. Relatability extends past key term use and user-generated content inclusion within marketing

material, it involves empathy, understanding and real-world awareness difficult to teach in a computer environment.

(6) **Personality.** The individual qualities and characteristics that form a person's unique character. Personality is a unique biological quality. Via content, people are able to express and convey their personalities which lead to emotionally triggered business gains stemmed from the audience and readership understanding and link to the content provided.

(7) **Business context.** Very few businesses have the same goals, objectives or requirements when they outsource expertise. The role of the marketing expert and content creator often incorporate some degree of business analysis, goal setting and situational understanding. This business understanding surpasses the data and informational levels of relationships and progresses into empathy. For content marketing and building to reflect distinct businesses, marketing messaging and company cultures, there is the necessity to empathise and identify with the company. This business contextualisation through empathy and added understanding are human qualities required to create differentiated content outputs.

(8) **Trust.** People trust other people more than any other reference point. This can be seen through the proliferation of review websites, independent product/service testing and reporting websites, aggregator websites, forums, and trusted (believed impartial) video content growth. To establish trust, you need to demonstrate and substantiate credibility and expertise, and while machines can assist people to do this, they cannot replace them.

(9) **Leadership.** There is a herd mentality that is ingrained in the behaviour traits of many audience personas. They (people) find it easier to make decisions based on following the path set by others. This practical leadership provision within content generally requires real-life people, displaying real-world purpose, positioning and benefits.

(10) **Authorship.** Also referred to as style, authorship explains the preference of writing style, approach and personalisation that not only differentiates content from one writer to the next but also has the ability to continually evolve (evolve over time and change based on environmental impact).

(11) **Authority.** Authoritative content has unique stand-alone value, setting it aside from competing examples, primarily based on the expertise provided by the person writing it. Expertise is almost impossible to replicate with any degree of credibility by anyone outside of the expert in question. Depth and completeness of problem-solving, practical experience-based reflection, as well as life skill reference points, all underpin this human factor for effective marketing content.

(12) **Accountability.** Taking on the accountability and ownership of content outputs and outcomes is an essential part of the content remit. Accountability cannot be attributed onto computers/machines and plays an important part of content quality controls and measures, as well as the analysis, reporting and ultimately the success from content produced.

(13) **Opinion.** Opinionated content drives social shares, comments and debate. Opinions can be controversial, valid and misplaced, but ultimately, they

have the ability to add another human aspect to content created which supports responsiveness and identification with people.

(14) **Video and visuals.** Great strides have been made notably within audio- and text-based fields of content creation; however, the main growing content digestion trends surround video, broader visual, and interactive content types. The ideation, collaboration, and creative structures required for these content types are much more human involved with far fewer data-driven opportunities at this point in time (notably within the ideation phases and visual/video content understanding by machines).

When looking at distinctive human roles over the next few years, there is an added value of an emphasis on the positions related to content building and curation throughout the process that become increasingly human dependant. Added to this are new roles which will become apparent as we discuss human/ computer collaboration later.

At this time, let us take a look at the increasingly important people positions and responsibilities in the content process, looking forward.

(1) **Content officers and chief content officer (CO).** Accountable for the quality and results delivered from the content, as well as the tone and voice of the final content outputs. Referred to as the lead and chief storytellers, COs pull everything together into one final piece in line with the company messaging, voice and cultural areas (consider business mission statements). As content becomes increasingly steered by data and reflective of audience wants and needs, the requirement for effective content officers and COs becomes increasingly apparent, to maintain, protect, and nurture the voice and quality of the brand. These roles are traditionally attributed to media outlets and content agencies; however, the growth of content importance, volume and company impact within businesses of all sizes, brings these (and other) role types and responsibilities into the mainstream market.

(2) **Editor/Chief Editor/Managing Editor.** The overarching project manager and ultimate person accountable for the delivery of complete content items and campaigns to deadline. The editorial roles stride between content project management and content quality (plus results). A trend within the more senior people positions in content now and more so moving forward is those that take on the answerability and culpability for the content results. This result orientation of roles and responsibilities are an important item to consider, as computers tend to remove some of the layers of human layers and certainly volumes, so the control measures and quality accountability requirements then tend to increase.

(3) **Commentator and listener.** At various stages in content curation and production, the content listeners and commentators (at junior and senior levels) take social and audience listening to the next stage of performance and business contribution. Think about these people as those having their ears closest to your audiences and providing insights and opportunity (plus threat insights) in situations where there is little, if any, current data to use.

The commentator element of this includes expertise imparting and audience building within valued persona group, trusted governing bodies, and trusted online and offline communities. The faces to companies and brands, the responsibilities and these people increase with the growing reliance of machine-fed content.

(4) **Technology leads.** Traditionally in the head of IT roles, technology leads are and will continue to become increasingly ingrained in the wider business and certainly content and marketing functions. These experts are managing the integrity, processing, use and improvement of all of the technology and data sources made available to create content. The integration, adoption, and maximisation of technology for content, marketing, plus other business uses (evaluation, reporting, more) all fall at the feet of technology officers and leads.

(5) **Outsourcing manager.** Business overheads will continue to migrate more towards technology (infrastructure, software, analytics, deep data plat-forms, etc.); however, there will be an increasing expert staffing need to fulfil new content campaigns, new business, ad hoc projects and supporting general delivery without the complete employment needs. This has already, and will create more, roles and responsibilities in the areas of freelance recruitment, management and other outsourcing fields.

(6) **Strategist.** Making sure that content being developed has a purpose (mission), is positioned according to the audience personas most important to the business, and demonstrates a clear vision, reflective of the business house styles and holistic company mission. Strategists will often lead the content marketing calendars, content action plans and roadmaps and ensure that strategy deployed meets the needs and expectations of business goals and objectives.

(7) **Researcher.** Similar and overlapping to some of the responsibilities of the content commentator and listener positions, the research led experts to work with all available information sources to build, refine, and fuel the ideation stages of content building. Frequently, this will include gathering new data, prioritising and justifying new content campaign focus.

(8) **Promotion specialists.** Content promotion when factoring in high quality and relevant placement (ordinarily on external websites, forums, social media groups and more) always comes back to relationship building. With added computer/machine investment, comes increased expectations for the results delivered and none more easily tracked than the promo-tion of the content. Link building, social sharing, engagement, and referral traffic are a few of the many result items associated to this area of performance.

(9) **Writers, proof readers and coordinators.** Content specialists are continually merging historically distinct roles and responsibility areas to reflect the increased efficiencies provided with machines. Added to this are the extra coordination and integration requirements to get buy-in and contribution from all of the experts and teams to produce content that stands up against the competition.

(10) **User experience experts.** Customer-centric content creation is more necessary than ever. User experience has become a prerequisite of content production, where it historically has been an optional extra. Content usability impacts micro and macro goal completions, as well as content function, shareability and other quality metrics, all required for content to performance anywhere near its true potential.

(11) **Channel writers.** A channel writer is, put simply, a content expert who has specialised skill sets unique to a content channel (examples include SEO, PPC, social media, email). Content produced for SEO would be vastly different to that created for a PPC landing page. The same holds true for people developing content for Twitter compared to LinkedIn, Quora or Reddit. The role of the generalist in marketing is dying out and becoming numerous specialist roles, something that has been identifiable certainly over the past decade or so, and one of the key budgetary advantages that companies can realise when they work with content, search and digital agencies for expertise provision.

On top of the previously detailed human content roles are increased functions for content governance and technical performance of content. These roles and responsibilities are in answer to added wider prioritisation and importance on speed of content delivery, ease of access to information, cross device compatibility, plus for governance, data protection, security and regulation requirements (including GDPR).

Human/Computer Collaboration

Taking a look into the new roles and responsibilities created by human and computer collaboration, we can see the evolution of both approaches to create many unique and exciting opportunities as well as new functions which otherwise wouldn't exist.

These newly formed and growing responsibility areas are some of the most exciting and perceived valuable by business, and you may be surprised to hear that quite a few of them have been around for some time now.

There is even a name for collaborative robot and human working, as this region has evolved to a stage, superseding previous benchmarks and expectations set (called 'co-bots').

The next few points focus on the changing approaches for content creation, looking forward with anticipated and increased human/computer working, plus a few of the new roles and responsibilities created by this collaborative environment.

(1) **Data Analysts.** Stemming from the traditional fields of mathematics, computer science and data analytics, marketing and content experts will all find themselves increasing the expertise levels closer towards that of a data scientist. With data trends, comparison, time series, and substantially

greater data involvement in all business decision-making, the perfect content writer and marketing professional will be a hybrid of many distinct parts. This will likely include (as it is already visible today) content, marketing, data (scientist and analyst), plus a few other areas such as PR and social media expertise. The heavy lifting of machines will enable this multiawareness increase as well as the more likely combined teams of multiple expertise. This is facilitated through employing more specialist content, data and marketing experts (with some overlapping expertise) and fewer content producers. This migration of reducing production-level staff and increasing efficiency gains from added machine emphasis, combined with increased senior (expertise/experience/capability) staff and added specialism areas to the business is the main trend appearing throughout.

(2) **Data Scientists.** Building on the data analytics roles that have been growing in SMB and larger companies as required business and marketing roles, a Data Scientist adds to that expertise area with a focus on solving complex problems, identifying the hidden problems that require attention and spotting the trends (untapped threats and opportunities) that business and marketing competitive advantages are created from. Data Scientists come from the same big data backgrounds seen with many Data Analytic/Analyst CVs; however, they often have more traditional data qualifications and experience-based seniority within the field.

(3) **Integrated services.** The days of isolated experts working on single channel, medium, or solo part of wider projects are long behind us. We discussed subtopics such as multipliers justifying increased integrated working, as well as the growing volume of user touchpoints and new technologies, reinforcing the functional needs to work integrated also. These increases will see role and responsibility changes that cater for the added importance of effective cross team, department and specialist areas, as well as likely, cross company integration (when factoring in external agencies and potential freelance staff fulfilment) success measurement, refinement and progression.

(4) **Brand usurpers.** It is not new that some of the most established business, industry leaders and brands can change over time, but what machines can bring to the table is speed and impact of SMB uprising. Consider the speed at which Uber took the taxi industry by storm and continues to grow globally. This has been fuelled by AI. Next Uber will become self-driving (driverless cars) and follow the 'production to senior' staff employment flow detailed in point (1). Uber is not an isolated case of a business progressing from relative obscurity into industry leader over a handful of years, and the costs of technological investment will only get more accessible as we see increasing advancements.

(5) **Technology experts.** Image, video, audio, and other types of content and marketing supportive technology (VR, AR, personal assistants, etc.) are becoming increasingly embedded into peoples lives. This provides new expertise areas tied to technology that you will begin to see filtering into the mainstream jobs. Creating VR and AR content is completely different to producing video content. The same can be said for building single page web

applications and infographics over content targeting personal assistant inclusion. The mixture of expertise required for such diverse technology type content creation, optimisation and marketing make it a clear choice for collaborative change.

(6) **Community content and audience building.** Too much of historical business and marketing content has been inwardly focussed. With deep data for audience understanding, content interaction and data-led success refinement, there is an increasing bridging between brand and community through the types of content created, plus the audience being an active participant within the content feedback loop. This regularly appears in traditional resource sections of websites but is becoming more engrained into the business and marketing culture as well as the business content mindset now. This is something that will only gain in momentum once increasing volumes of companies begin to identify the gains as with shortening sales cycles, increasing upselling and wider brand reach and engagement metrics. Part of this changing approach includes the tailoring of content and increased niche persona and audience access by genuine, real-world understanding and pain point resolution by business.

(7) **Text migration.** There will be added creative expert (content and marketing) roles required to account for the increasing move towards alternative content preferences, away from text. Driving influences for this include the mobile first prioritisation of content in Google from 2018. The change in mobile use and smartphone technology, plus the increased integrated SERPs use of image and video content means that mixed content types may well outgrow traditional text as the preferred digestion approach by consumers.

(8) **Screenless.** Screenless user search, discovery and content delivery (personal assistants and home speakers a good example of this in action) increase the business case for targeting screenless marketing devices. As you would anticipate, this changes the technical expertise requirements as well as the wider awareness for creating content that is able to deliver results in newer and growing opportunity areas. I would expect the next five years to see screenless search accounting for 40% or more of total search engine marketing.

(9) **Experiential and interactive.** We are already experiencing the rise of and growth in experiential retail. This is primarily (but not exclusively) millennially driven, reflecting the younger consumers' need to have a more engaging experience. This can include increased offline/online integration, mobile apps usage and Virtual Reality bridging the online/offline buying environment. When building on the results and value elements of marketing content, ensure that expert attention and repurposing opportunity includes dynamic capabilities. The more this dynamism becomes the business content norm, the more increased gains will be delivered through content and marketing differentiation and perceived value.

(10) **Hyperlocal.** The use of wearable technology (smartwatches, mobile phones, personal trackers, fitness devices and more) empowers companies to target

users with increase immediacy and hyper locality. An example of this in action is Google Beacons and the hyperlocal retail experiences. Companies can use hyperlocal audience tracking and engagement to deliver highly personalised and immediate marketing signals to trigger user actions. This can include sending SMS updates to people as they walk within a few metres of your store or providing marketing messaging (smart discounts and product information) as people look at products on shelves within your shop. This type of action-based marketing, product and content positioning could be the game changer that revitalises the decline in physical retail outlets and stores, combining technology with real-world, differentiation and application, to increase the value given to the user.

(11) **Testing and experimentation.** Fundamental components for any data-driven methodology, hypothesis testing, A/B, multivariant and other forms of testing and experiments will move from optional focus and intermittent application into key audience and result-orientated action plans and performance roadmaps. Repurposing content and refining content for business and marketing gains are paramount expertise items and expect this to substantially increase over the next few years.

(12) **Data curation.** Human/robot collaboration will facilitate greater content curation and volume-based content provision, at a level never seen before. It is a known fact that companies are creating more content than ever before, and people are respectively consuming more, so the challenge then moves onto the ability to facilitate meaningful content curation and delivery to the increased scale without detriment to quality. The increased advantages of data understanding and efficiency for prescribing content building are second to none when combining the data processing and AI from computers with the emotive and experiential humanistic qualities of people. A marketing channel likely to see large increases in tactical deployment from this include native advertising.

(13) **Digital story-making and storytelling.** Driven by data and delivered on varying digital marketing platforms, digital story-making and storytelling is growing in traction, and even offline and more traditional marketing mediums strive to include digital and data within their approaches to increase results. Evidence of this in practice can be seen with shorter form content creation and repurposing for digital mediums; increasing use of video, VR, AR and other screenless search and discovery interactions; plus the reduced digital barriers to entry combined with increased big data access.

(14) **Framework automation.** The first value brought by machines always impacts efficiencies. This can be seen as much in the new technology machine age as it was in the early movements from human labour and power moving to steam power. People understand efficiency and use it to allocate budget as well as to forecast ROI. By automating the data-driven elements of content writing (putting together the bulk of the body content for articles, blog posts, news stories, etc.), the standardised elements of content productions become faster and increasingly scalable. The monotony between ideation,

research and article building become automated, so the expertise, creativity, passion, opinion and other human qualities can be applied.

(15) **Engagement frequency.** Interestingly, while the levels of engagement and interactions between companies and consumers will increase, the amount of time people spend digesting business and marketing content will likely remain consistent (or potentially reduce). The logic supporting this statement is that people are becoming increasingly concise in their new content tolerance, meaning that content is becoming easier to skim read, and in lots of situations shorter form content being published. Added to this is the repurposing of salient content messaging and takeaway opinions on micro blogging platforms and social media sites, enabling most content awareness to be facilitated with minimum content reading. Consumer movement from desktop to mobile and content type migration from text to image, audio and video all help shape the engagement towards shorter and more frequent touchpoints.

(16) **Value-based clustering.** The grouping of content to provide increased expertise, authority and trust all tied around a persona type, and/or topic area, has grown in popularity over the past several years, with the changing technology opportunities, enabling extra interactivity and experiential value. These content hubs/clusters/sections of value will continue to grow in application and results derived over the years to follow with added emphasis and on the community and experience aspect of them.

(17) **Added collaboration roles.** In this chapter, the topic of increased human needs was discussed, and this will lead to new role creation necessary to maximise the outputs from collaborative working between humans/robots. The areas expected to be impacted the most initially would be:

- Proof readers and content coordinators
- Usability and user experience specialists
- Data Scientists and Analysts
- Channel writers and content promotion experts
- Content and marketing strategists
- Ideation specialists and researchers
- Technology leads
- Senior integration account managers/campaign leads
- More

Chapter Summary

This guide has steered you through all of the fundamental areas of data-driven marketing and business content.

We started by introducing data-driven content and setting the data situation for businesses.

This naturally led onto understanding the data ecosystem, putting in place the first of many content building frameworks and a practical look at revitalising your current business content.

The concepts of ML and AI were discussed within the context of content building, and we delved into the world of data collection and management, including the role that GDPR has to play.

Chapter 4 led you through the processes of transforming data into content, audience personas and creating content action plans.

By the halfway point of this practical business content guide, we started to dig deeper into why your marketing content is failing; overcoming content pain points, integrating marketing mediums and creating successful content for distinct marketing channels.

The latter part of this guide focussed on getting over content barriers, making the most out of all your existing content and the provision of practical and repeatable approaches and frameworks for producing more effective content for marketing.

Chapter 9 led us from the content creation and ideation stages covered earlier in the book, towards evaluating content success; setting benchmarks, goals and objectives, choosing the best KPIs and reporting on results.

In this final chapter, we took a look forward at the future of data-driven content; the roles that machine and humans will fulfil plus the expected growth of human/robot collaboration.

Definitions

- SWOT analysis: standing for internal strengths and weaknesses, as well as its external opportunities and threats, this (SWOT) is a form of analysis completed as part of targeted or broader situational based business analysis. SWOT analysis has many applications and often gets included within approaches for strategic planning.
- Co-bots: the term is used to describe the effective collaborative working robots which can interact with humans to derive added business benefit. Co-bots are also referred to as cobots and co-robots.
- Hyperlocal marketing: as the name suggests, this is a highly targeted form of local business marketing targeting within any given region (normally sub-regions). Hyperlocal examples could include marketing to a city, county and even small region for very refined business niche success.
- Native advertising: often found within social media settings, there are paid adverts which appear to take on the look, feel and design of the surrounding format. The purpose of native advertising is to appear to be non-sales-based media, supporting greater perceived relevancy, trust and associated gains (CTR, CPA and more).

References

There are many reference points that I've used historically and as part of my own investigations into the material created in this business guide.

Those that have been most memorable at the time of writing this textbook are listed here.

Please note: as with all external resources cited, I have no control over the content, information or opinions provided, and only suggest them as potential practical sources for facilitating the furthering of your own investigations into the subject matters covered.

BrandWatch. (2018). *39 Fascinating and incredible YouTube statistics.* Retrieved from https://www.brandwatch.com/blog/39-youtube-stats/.

Content Marketing Institute. (2016). *10 Content marketing roles for the next 10 years.* Retrieved from https://contentmarketinginstitute.com/2016/10/content-marketing-roles/.

Content Marketing Institute. (2018). *Will Artificial Intelligence replace manual content creation?* Retrieved from https://contentmarketinginstitute.com/2017/03/artificial-intelligence-manual-creation/.

Convince and Convert. (2018). *4 Telling trends that predict the future of content marketing.* Retrieved from https://www.convinceandconvert.com/content-marketing/4-telling-trends-that-predict-the-future-of-content-marketing/.

EU GDPR.org. (2018a). *GDPR key changes.* Retrieved from https://eugdpr.org/the-regulation/.

EU GDPR.org. (2018b). *GDPR FAQs.* Retrieved from https://eugdpr.org/the-regulation/gdpr-faqs/.

European Commission. (2018a). *2018 reform of EU data protection rules.* Retrieved from https://ec.europa.eu/commission/priorities/justice-and-fundamental-rights/data-protection/2018-reform-eu-data-protection-rules_en#abouttheregulationand dataprotection.

European Commission. (2018b). *Data protection.* Retrieved from https://ec.europa.eu/justice/smedataprotect/index_en.htm.

Forbes. (2018). *IBM CEO Rometty proposes 'Watson's Law': AI in everything.* Retrieved from https://www.forbes.com/sites/adrianbridgwater/2018/03/20/ibm-ceo-rometty-proposes-watsons-law-ai-in-everything/#b4590e14d087.

Google. (2018a). *Machine Learning Crash Course | Google developers.* Retrieved from https://developers.google.com/machine-learning/crash-course/.

Google. (2018b). *Our products | Google.* Retrieved from https://www.google.co.uk/about/products/.

Google. (2018c). *Google marketing platform.* Retrieved from https://marketing platform.google.com/about/optimize/.

Google. (2018d). *Analytics help – About demographics and interests.* Retrieved from https://support.google.com/analytics/answer/2799357?hl=en.

Google Analytics. (2018). *Dimensions & metrics explorer.* Retrieved from https://developers.google.com/analytics/devguides/reporting/core/dimsmets.

Google Beacon Platform. (2018). *Mark up the world using beacons.* Retrieved from https://developers.google.com/beacons/.

HubSpot. (2018). *5 SMART goal examples that'll make you a better marketer.* Retrieved from https://blog.hubspot.com/marketing/smart-goal-examples.

IBM. (2018). *Bag data analytics.* Retrieved from https://www.ibm.com/analytics/hadoop/big-data-analytics.

IBM Big Data and Analytics Hub. (2018). *The Four V's of big data.* Retrieved from https://www.ibmbigdatahub.com/infographic/four-vs-big-data.

IBM Consumer Products Industry Blog. (2013). *2.5 Quintillion bytes of data created every day. How does CPG & Retail manage it?* Retrieved from https://www.ibm.com/blogs/insights-on-business/consumer-products/2-5-quintillion-bytes-of-data-created-every-day-how-does-cpg-retail-manage-it/.

Keystone Virtual. (2018). *What is an audience persona and why do they matter?* Retrieved from https://keystonevirtual.com/what-is-an-audience-persona/.

Marketing Profs. (2017). *The incredible amount of data generated online every minute.* Retrieved from https://www.marketingprofs.com/charts/2017/32531/the-incredible-amount-of-data-generated-online-every-minute-infographic.

McKinsey & Company. (2018). *How companies are using big data and analytics.* Retrieved from https://www.mckinsey.com/business-functions/mckinsey-analytics/our-insights/how-companies-are-using-big-data-and-analytics.

Meltwater. (2018). *10 Reasons your organization needs an internal newsletter.* Retrieved from https://www.meltwater.com/blog/11-reasons-your-organization-needs-an-internal-newsletter/.

Moz. (2015). *What is Google RankBrain?* Retrieved from https://moz.com/learn/seo/google-rankbrain.

Moz. (2016). *4 Ways copywriting can boost your E-commerce conversion rates.* Retrieved from https://moz.com/blog/4-ways-copywriting-can-help-your-ecommerce-conversion-rates.

Nielsen Norman Group. (2017). *F-shaped pattern of reading on the web: Misunderstood, but still relevant (even on mobile).* Retrieved from https://www.nngroup.com/articles/f-shaped-pattern-reading-web-content/.

Omnicore Agency. (2018). *YouTube by the numbers: Stats, demographics & fun facts.* Retrieved from https://www.omnicoreagency.com/youtube-statistics/.

Project Smart. (2017). *Smart goals.* Retrieved from https://www.projectsmart.co.uk/smart-goals.php.

Science Soft. (2018). *4 Types of data analytics to improve decision-making.* Retrieved from https://www.scnsoft.com/blog/4-types-of-data-analytics.

Search Engine Journal. (2018). *The future of SEO & content: Can AI replace human writers?* Retrieved from https://www.searchenginejournal.com/ai-vs-human-seo-content/268629/.

State of Digital. (2017). *Screenless search marketing essentials – Your practical guide.* Retrieved from https://www.stateofdigital.com/screenless-search-marketing-essentials-practical-guide/.

The Drum. (2018). *How to prepare your content for voice search.* Retrieved from https://www.thedrum.com/opinion/2018/11/08/how-prepare-your-content-voice-search.

Wikipedia. (2018a). *Big data.* Retrieved from https://en.wikipedia.org/wiki/Big_data.

Wikipedia. (2018b). *Machine Learning.* Retrieved from https://en.wikipedia.org/wiki/Machine_learning.

Wikipedia. (2018c). *AI for good.* Retrieved from https://en.wikipedia.org/wiki/AI_for_Good.

Wikipedia. (2018d). *Workflow.* Retrieved from https://en.wikipedia.org/wiki/Workflow.

YouTube. (2018). *YouTube studio.* Retrieved from https://studio.youtube.com.

Index